The Hulton Getty Picture Collection

1960s

Decades of the 20th Century
Dekaden des 20. Jahrhunderts
Décennies du XXe siècle

Nick Yapp

KÖNEMANN

First published in 1998 by Könemann Verlagsgesellschaft mbH, Bonner Straße 126, D-50968 Köln

This book was produced by The Hulton Getty Picture Collection Limited,
Unique House, 21–31 Woodfield Road, London W9 2BA

For Könemann:
Production director: Detlev Schaper
Managing editor: Sally Bald
Project editor: Susanne Hergarden
Assistants: Sabine Gerber, Markus Nelle
Production assistant: Nicola Leurs
German translation: Ellen Küppers
French translation: Francine Rey
Contributing editor: Annick Schmidt

For Hulton Getty:
Art director: Michael Rand
Design: Ian Denning
Managing editor: Annabel Else
Picture editor: Ali Khoja
Picture research: Alex Linghorn
Editor: James Hughes
Proof reader: Elisabeth Ihre
Scanning: Austin Bryan
Production: Robert Gray
Special thanks: Leon Meyer,
Téa Aganovic and Antonia Hille

Typesetting by Greiner & Reichel Fotosatz. Colour separation by R&B Creative Services Group
Printed and bound by Sing Cheong Printing Co. Ltd., Hong Kong, China

ISBN 3-8290-0523-7
10 9 8 7 6

Frontispiece: Dr Timothy Leary and his wife Rosemary on their honeymoon
at Laguna Beach, California, 12 February 1968. The image is one of great
purity, but to many Leary was the evil advocate of LSD and Marijuana.

Frontispiz: Dr. Timothy Leary und seine Frau Rosemary während ihrer
Flitterwochen in Laguna Beach, Kalifornien, 12. Februar 1968. Das Bild
wirkt rein und unschuldig, doch viele hielten Leary für den teuflischen
Hohepriester von LSD und Marihuana.

Frontispice : Le Dr. Timothy Leary et sa femme Rosemary en lune de miel à
Laguna Beach, Californie, 12 février 1968. Cette image est d'une grande
pureté mais, pour beaucoup, Leary était l'avocat du diable, le défenseur du
LSD et de la marijuana.

Contents / Inhalt / Sommaire

Introduction

The Sixties saw good and evil harvests from the seeds sown in the previous decade. In South Africa, apartheid produced the Sharpeville massacre and the assassination of Verwoerd. Castro's revolution in Cuba produced the Bay of Pigs fiasco. JFK was inaugurated President in 1961 and in a short time redefined the aspirations of an increasingly politicized population. The momentum created by the civil rights movement swept through the United States in the Sixties. In the ensuing turmoil Martin Luther King was gunned down; there were race riots in LA, Chicago, New York and Cleveland; and Malcolm X and Black Power burst upon the scene.

In Britain, the golden days of Prime Minister "Supermac" Macmillan and his consumer-driven conservatism were abruptly brought to an end by the Profumo scandal. In China, Mao Zedong unleashed the Red Guard. In Africa, Ian Smith led his Rhodesian settlers in an ultimately hopeless attempt to hang on to white power. Nelson Mandela was jailed for life. Jomo Kenyatta led his people to independence. The Greeks threw out their king. Violent death was the fate of Che Guevara in Bolivia, Adolf Eichmann in Israel, and the defenceless villagers of My Lai in Vietnam. Marilyn Monroe overdosed. Elvis Presley overate.

In 1968 all hell broke loose. The Soviet empire was shaken but not thawed by the Prague Spring. Paris almost had yet another revolution. Bobby Kennedy was assassinated. Civil war broke out in Biafra. There were riots in Chicago at the Democrat Convention. Black athletes gave the Black Power salute at the Mexico Olympics. In Europe and the States, schools and colleges became centres of anarchy, liberalism, pop culture and an ill-defined 'Red menace'. The Beatles endlessly repeated that 'All You Need Is Love', but it wasn't enough. Flower Power may have been initially beautiful; eventually it was ineffective.

All was conflict and argument. There were those who wished to extend higher education to all and sundry, while others preached the doctrine of deschooling. Drugs were good, drugs were bad. The Bomb was 'the great deterrent' or the great monster. Some reckoned Kennedy had saved the world by not backing down in the Cuban Missile Crisis. Others believed Khrushchev had saved the world because he did back down.

Disasters struck everywhere. At Aberfan, Wales, a vast pile of mud and slag slithered down a hillside and killed 144 people, 141 of them children. Florence was flooded. The oil tanker *Torrey Canyon* ran aground off Land's End, to give the world a taste of pollution to come.

Skopje was wrecked by an earthquake in the Balkans. The Ronan Point tower block collapsed in London. The Apollo Mission ended in tragedy at Cape Canaveral.

But there were also successes. The jumbo jet was born. Concorde roared through its maiden flight. The *QE2* ocean liner kept alive dreams of a romantic seafaring past, and Sir Francis Chichester sailed alone around the world. Yuri Gagarin became the first man in space. James Bond became the last word in sexy sophistication. Rudolf Nureyev danced his way into Western hearts and found asylum there. Bob Dylan reckoned the answer to it all was 'Blowing in the Wind', but many women found a better answer in the Pill.

Einführung

Die sechziger Jahre hatten in mancher Hinsicht ein schweres Erbe der vorangegangenen Dekade anzutreten. Die Apartheidspolitik in Südafrika gipfelte in dem Massaker von Sharpeville und in der Ermordung von Hendrik Verwoerd. Castros Revolution auf Kuba folgte das Schweinebucht-Fiasko. JFK wurde 1961 in das Amt des Präsidenten eingesetzt und definierte in kürzester Zeit die Ziele einer mehr und mehr politisierten Öffentlichkeit neu. Ein Ruck ging in den sechziger Jahren duch die Vereinigten Staaten, der durch die Bürgerrechtsbewegung ausgelöst wurde. In seiner Folge wurde Martin Luther King erschossen; es gab Rassenunruhen in Los Angeles, Chicago, New York und Cleveland; und Malcolm X und die Black Power-Bewegung erschienen auf der Bühne.

In Großbritannien sorgte der Profumo-Skandal für Schlagzeilen und bedeutete für den Premierminister Macmillan, „Supermac", und seinen konsumorientierten Konservatismus das abrupte politische Aus. In China festigte Mao Tse-tung mit Hilfe der Roten Truppen seine Macht. In Afrika trugen die weißen Kolonialherren in Rhodesien unter Führung von Ian Smith einen letzten verzweifelten Kampf um ihre Vormachtstellung aus. Nelson Mandela wurde zu lebenslanger Haft verurteilt. Jomo Kenyatta führte sein Land in die Unabhängigkeit. Die Griechen verbannten ihren König. Ein gewaltsamer Tod war das Schicksal Che Guevaras in Bolivien, Adolf Eichmanns in Israel und der wehrlosen Opfer des vietnamesischen Dorfes My Lai. Marilyn Monroe starb an einer Überdosis. Elvis Presley überaß sich.

1968 brach die Hölle los. Der Prager Frühling brachte die Sowjetunion ins Wanken, zwang sie aber nicht in die Knie. In Paris gab es beinahe wieder eine Revolution. Bob Kennedy wurde erschossen. In Biafra brach ein Bürgerkrieg aus. In Chicago kam es zu Rassenunruhen während des Parteitags der Demokraten. Schwarze Sportler nahmen die Olympischen Spiele von Mexiko zum Anlaß, um den Black Power-Gruß zu zeigen. In Europa und den Vereinigten

Staaten verwandelten sich die Schulen und Universitäten zu Keimzellen der Anarchie, der Liberalität, der Popkultur und einer falsch eingeschätzten „Roten Bedrohung". Die Beatles verkündeten immer wieder: „All You Need Is Love", aber das reichte nicht. Flower Power war zwar gut gemeint; war aber am Ende doch nicht effektiv.

Es war eine Zeit des Konflikts und des Für und Widers. Die einen forderten bessere Bildungschancen für alle, die anderen proklamierten die Verweigerung des akademischen Systems. Drogen waren gut, Drogen waren schlecht. Die Atombombe galt entweder als „die große Abschreckung", oder als das große Monster. Die einen feierten Kennedy, weil er während der Kubakrise hart geblieben war. Die anderen glaubten, daß Chruschtschow der Held sei, weil er nachgegeben hatte.

Die Medien meldeten Katastrophen in allen Teilen der Welt. In Aberfan, Wales, ging ein Erdrutsch nieder und begrub 144 Menschen unter sich, 141 davon waren Kinder. Florenz wurde überschwemmt. Der Öltanker *Torrey Canyon* lief beim Kap Land's End auf Grund und gab der Welt einen ersten Vorgeschmack auf die Umweltzerstörungen, die noch kommen sollten.

Ein Erdbeben im Balkan zerstörte die Stadt Skopje. In London stürzte der Ronan-Point-Tower ein. In Cape Canaveral endete die Apollo-Weltraummission in einer Tragödie.

Doch es gab auch erfreuliche Meldungen. Der Jumbo-Jet war aus der Taufe gehoben. Die *Concorde* hatte ihren Jungfernflug. Der Ozeandampfer *Queen Elizabeth II* nährte die Träume von einer romantischen Hochseefahrt, und Sir Francis Chichester umsegelte allein die Welt. Yuri Gagarin schwebte als erster Mensch durch die Weiten des Weltraums. James Bond wurde zum Inbegriff der Attraktivität. Rudolf Nurejew tanzte sich in die Herzen des Westens und fand Asyl. Bob Dylans musikalische Antwort auf alles lautete: „Blowing in the Wind", doch viele Frauen hatten eine bessere Antwort gefunden: die Pille.

Introduction

Les années soixante avaient semé les graines de récoltes qui allaient s'avérer bonnes ou mauvaises dans les années soixante. En Afrique du Sud, l'apartheid aboutit au massacre de Sharpeville et à l'assassinat de Verwoerd. A Cuba, la révolution castriste engendra le fiasco de la baie des Cochons. John Fitzgerald Kennedy entra à la Maison Blanche en 1961 et en un court laps de temps, il redéfinit les aspirations d'une population de plus en plus politisée. La dynamique créée par le mouvement des droits civils se répandit à travers les Etats-Unis au cours des années soixante. Une période de troubles s'ensuivit. Martin Luther King fut abattu. Des émeutes raciales éclatèrent à Los Angeles, Chicago, New York et Cleveland, catapultant Malcolm X et le Black Power sur le devant de la scène.

En Grande-Bretagne, le scandale Profumo sonna abruptement le glas des beaux jours de « Supermac », le Premier ministre Macmillan, et de son conservatisme pro-consommation. En Chine, Mao Tsê-toung lâcha les « gardes rouges » à la poursuite des opposants au régime. En Afrique, Ian Smith entraîna les colons rhodésiens dans une dernière tentative désespérée afin de maintenir le pouvoir blanc. Nelson Mandela fut condamné à la prison à vie. Jomo Kenyatta mena son pays à l'indépendance. Les Grecs expulsèrent leur roi. Che Guevara en Bolivie et les habitants sans défense du village de My Lai au Viêt-nam moururent de mort violente, tout comme Adolf Eichmann en Israël. Marilyn Monroe succomba à une overdose. Elvis Presley devint boulimique.

En 1968, les cieux se déchaînèrent. L'empire soviétique fut ébranlé par le « printemps de Prague » mais resta néanmoins intact. Paris vécut une nouvelle révolution ou presque. Bobby Kennedy fut assassiné. La guerre civile éclata au Biafra. Il y eut des émeutes pendant la Convention démocrate à Chicago. Aux Jeux olympiques de Mexico, des athlètes noirs font le salut du Black Power, le poing levé. En Europe et aux Etats-Unis, les écoles et les universités étaient devenues les foyers de l'anarchie, du libéralisisme, de la culture pop et tout ce qui était apparenté à la « menace rouge ». Les Beatles répétaient sans fin « All you need is love » mais cela ne suffisait pas. Le mouvement hippie « flower power » qui avait tant séduit à ses débuts parut en fin de compte plutôt inefficace.

Tout n'était que conflits et controverses. Il y avait ceux qui revendiquaient une éducation supérieure accessible à tous, tandis que d'autres défendaient l'école alternative. Les drogues, c'était bien pour certains, mal pour d'autres. La bombe atomique était considérée comme la meilleure des armes de dissuasion ou, au contraire, comme une arme monstrueuse. Pour certains, Kennedy avait sauvé le monde en ne cédant pas durant la crise des missiles cubains. Pour d'autres, Khrouchtchev avait sauvé le monde justement parce qu'il avait cédé.

Des catastrophes firent des ravages aux quatre coins du monde. A Aberfan, aux Pays de Galles, une énorme plaque de boue et de terril glissa en bas d'une colline, tuant 144 personnes dont 141 enfants. Florence fut inondée. Le pétrolier *Torrey Canyon* s'échoua à Land's End en Angleterre, donnant au monde un avant-goût des pollutions à venir.

Dans les Balkans, Skopje fut dévastée par un tremblement de terre. A Londres, la tour Ronan Point s'effondra. A Cap Canaveral, la mission Apollo se termina tragiquement.

Heureusement, il y eut aussi des réussites. On assista à la naissance du Jumbo, un avion géant, et aux premiers vols d'essai du Concorde. Le *Queen Elizabeth II* entretenait la légende romantique et nostalgique du voyage sur les mers et Sir Francis Chichester accomplissait son tour du monde en solitaire. Youri fut le premier homme dans l'espace. James Bond devint le symbole de l'élégance sexy. Le danseur Rudolf Noureïev qui avait conquis le coeur des Occidentaux se réfugia à l'Ouest. Quant à Bob Dylan, sa réponse à tout ça était « Blowing in the Wind » mais, pour de nombreuses femmes, la meilleure des réponses fut la pilule.

1. Movers and shakers
Spieler und Gegenspieler
Progressistes et agitateurs

John Fitzgerald Kennedy, the 35th president of the United States, 31 May 1961. From his inauguration to his assassination, Kennedy led his country for just 1,037 days, but his impact on politics in the Sixties was immense.

John Fitzgerald Kennedy war der 35. Präsident der Vereinigten Staaten von Amerika, 31. Mai 1961. Von seiner Einsetzung bis zu seiner Ermordung dauerte seine Amtszeit nur 1.037 Tage, trotzdem beeinflußte er die Politik der sechziger Jahre nachhaltig.

John Fitzgerald Kennedy, 35e président des Etats-Unis, 31 mai 1961. De son investiture à son assassinat, Kennedy gouverna son pays pendant 1 037 jours seulement, mais son influence sur la politique des années soixante fut immense.

1. Movers and shakers
Spieler und Gegenspieler
Progressistes et agitateurs

Not since the 1840s or the 1920s had there been such tumultuous political upheavals throughout the world. The alphabet of instability began with Algeria and apartheid, went on to Biafra and the Berlin Wall, the Congo and Cuba, and worked its way right through to Vietnam. The dramas were tragic, exciting, uplifting, depressing, shocking and continuous.

At the beginning of the decade Eisenhower was still president of the USA and Churchill remained a senior statesman in Britain. By the time the Sixties whirled to their end, both were dead, Nixon had sweated his way into the White House, Ho Chi Minh had died, and de Gaulle was a spent force.

There were those who had their brief spell of fame and glory – Alexander Dubček, Che Guevara, Ian Smith. There were those who stayed the distance – Mao Zedong and President Tito looked set to last forever. And there were some names that were never out of the headlines. JFK was killed in 1963, his brother Bobby five years later. Chappaquiddick dented Edward Kennedy's career in July 1969, and four months later old Joe Kennedy died.

Nelson Mandela began his 26 years in prison in 1964. Two years later, the man who put him there, Hendrik Verwoerd was stabbed to death by a white extremist.

Die politischen Umwälzungen und Tumulte jener Zeit erreichten überall auf der Welt eine Größenordnung, wie es sie seit den 1840ern oder 1920ern nicht mehr gegeben hatte. Das Alphabet der Instabilitäten begann mit Algerien und der Apartheid, ging dann weiter zu Biafra und der Berliner Mauer, dem Kongo und Kuba und reicht bis zu Vietnam. Die Dramen waren tragisch, aufregend, spannend, niederschlagend, schockierend und dauerhaft.

Anfang des Jahrzehnts war Eisenhower noch der Präsident der Vereinigten Staaten, und Churchill zählte in England weiterhin zu den führenden Staatsmännern. Als sich die sechziger

Jahre dem Ende zuneigten, waren beide tot, Nixon hatte sich den Weg ins Weiße Haus gebahnt, Ho Chi Minh war gestorben, und de Gaulle hatte seine politische Macht verloren.

Einige wie Alexander Dubček, Che Guevara oder Ian Smith genossen für einen kurzen Moment ihre Bekanntheit und ihren Ruhm. Es gab auch jene, die sich auf Distanz hielten – Mao Tse-tung und Präsident Tito schienen einen Platz für die Ewigkeit zu haben. Andere Namen hingegen kamen nie aus den Schlagzeilen. JFK wurde 1963 in Dallas ermordet, sein Bruder Bobby wurde fünf Jahre später getötet. Chappaquiddick beendete im Juli 1969 Edward Kennedys Karriere, und vier Monate später starb das Oberhaupt des Clans, Joe Kennedy.

Nelson Mandela begann 1964 seine 26jährige Haftstrafe zu verbüßen. Zwei Jahre später starb der Mann, der ihn verurteilt hatte, Hendrik Verwoerd, an den Messerstichen eines weißen Extremisten.

Il n'y avait pas eu, depuis les années 1840 ou 1920, autant de soulèvements et de tumultes politiques à travers le monde. L'alphabet de l'instabilité commençait avec l'Algérie et l'apartheid, continuait avec le Biafra et le mur de Berlin, le Congo et Cuba et se déclinait ainsi jusqu'à la lettre V pour Viêt-nam. Les drames qui s'ensuivaient étaient tour à tour tragiques, passionnants, porteurs d'espoir, démoralisants, choquants et sans fin.

Au début de la décennie, Eisenhower était encore président des Etats-Unis et Churchill un homme d'Etat important en Grande-Bretagne. A la fin des années soixante, les deux hommes étaient morts, Nixon s'était frayé un chemin jusqu'à la Maison Blanche, Hô Chi Minh était décédé et de Gaulle un homme au pouvoir usé.

Certains, tels Alexandre Dubček, Che Guevara ou Ian Smith, connurent un bref moment de notoriété et de gloire. Il y avait aussi ceux qui savaient tenir la distance comme Mao Tsé-toung et le président Tito qui semblaient en place pour toujours. Il y eut aussi des noms qui faisaient sans cesse la une des journaux. John Kennedy fut assassiné en 1963, son frère, Bobby, cinq ans plus tard. Chappaquiddick ruina la carrière d'Edward Kennedy en juillet 1969 et quatre mois plus tard, le vieux Joe Kennedy mourait.

En 1964, Nelson Mandela purgeait la première année d'une peine de prison qui allait durer 26 ans. Deux ans plus tard, l'homme qui l'avait condamné, Hendrik Verwoerd, était poignardé à mort par un extrémiste blanc.

A heated exchange during the Cold War. Vice-President Nixon of the United States gives the finger to the Soviet premier, Nikita Khrushchev, in the aftermath of the U2 spy plane crisis, 1960.

Gereizte Stimmung während des Kalten Krieges. Nixon, Vizepräsident der USA, droht dem sowjetischen Staatschef Nikita Chruschtschow im Anschluß an die Krise im Rahmen der U2-Spionageflugzeuge, 1960.

Echange verbal très vif durant la guerre froide. Nixon, le vice-président des Etats-Unis, porte un doigt accusateur sur Nikita Khrouchtchev, le premier secrétaire soviétique, suite à la crise des avions d'espionnage U2, 1960.

A happier handshake. President John Kennedy and Khrushchev meet at the US Embassy in Vienna in June 1961. Their apparent friendship was totally false. Two months earlier, relations between the USA and the Soviet Union had been strained to the limit by the Bay of Pigs incident in Cuba.

Ein Handschlag zwischen Staatsmännern. Präsident John Kennedy und Chruschtschow treffen sich im Juni 1961 in der US-Botschaft in Wien. Doch der Schein freundschaftlicher Beziehungen trügt. Zwei Monate zuvor hatten die beiden Supermächte ihr Verhältnis durch den Vorfall in der Schweinebucht auf's Äußerste strapaziert.

Poignée de mains plus cordiale. Rencontre entre le président John Kennedy et Khrouchtchev à l'ambassade américaine à Vienne en juin 1961. Leur amitié apparente était totalement feinte. Deux mois plus tôt, suite à l'incident de la baie des Cochons à Cuba, les relations américano-soviétiques étaient plus tendues que jamais.

The new attraction, 1961. Sightseers climb atop a tour bus to look over the newly built Berlin Wall. It stayed there for another 28 years.

Die neue Attraktion, 1961. Schaulustige klettern auf einen Bus, um einen Blick über die soeben errichtete Berliner Mauer zu werfen. Sie sollte noch 28 Jahre stehen.

La nouvelle attraction, 1961. Des badauds montent sur le toit de leur bus pour regarder par-dessus le mur de Berlin, érigé depuis peu. Il allait tenir encore 28 ans.

Hot and cold – hot. In the warm days of summer, Nikita Khrushchev and President Josip Tito of Yugoslavia relax together on the *Podgorka*, during a sight-seeing trip along the Istrian coast, 26 August 1963. It was another uneasy friendship.

Heiß oder kalt? Heiß. An einem warmen Sommertag entspannen sich Nikita Chruschtschow und der jugoslawische Präsident Josip Tito auf dem Deck der *Podgorka* während eines Ausflugs entlang der Istrischen Küste, 26. August 1963. Diese Freundschaft war ebenso problematisch.

Chaud ou froid? Chaud. Par une belle journée d'été, Nikita Khrouchtchev et Josip Tito, le président de la Yougoslavie, se détendent sur le *Podgorka*, lors d'une sortie en bateau le long de la côte d'Istrie, 26 août 1963. Cette amitié était, elle aussi, difficile.

Hot and cold – cold. Khrushchev and the president of Finland,
Urho Kekkonen (left), meet dressed for a hunting trip in
December 1963. Each was probably the other's preferred kill.

Heiß oder kalt? Kalt. Nikita Chruschtschow und der finnische
Staatspräsident Urho Kekkonen (links) treffen sich im Dezember
1963 zu einem Jagdausflug. Sie hätten sich wahrscheinlich am
liebsten gegenseitig zur Zielscheibe genommen.

Chaud ou froid? Froid. Rencontre entre Khrouchtchev et
le président de la Finlande, Urho Kekkonen (à gauche), prêts
pour une partie de chasse, décembre 1963. Chacun aurait
probablement volontiers fait de l'autre sa proie favorite.

Khrushchev and Polish president Wladyslaw Gomulka in jovial mood at the United Nations, New York, 22 September 1960. Two weeks later, Khrushchev pounded his desk in rage at the UN, accused by a Philippine diplomat of depriving Poland and others of 'political and civil rights'.

Chruschtschow und der polnische Staatspräsident Wladyslaw Gomulka zeigen sich bei einem Treffen der Vereinten Nationen in bester Stimmung, New York, 22. September 1960. Zwei Wochen später schlug Chruschtschow wutentbrannt mit der Faust auf den Tisch, als ihn ein philippinischer Diplomat beschuldigte, Polen und andere Staaten „politisch und in deren Bürgerrechten", zu unterdrücken.

Khrouchtchev et le président polonais Wladyslaw Gomulka tout sourire aux Nations Unies, New York, 22 septembre 1960. Deux semaines plus tard, Khrouchtchev frappait de rage sa table à l'ONU, un diplomate philippin l'accusait de priver la Pologne et d'autres pays de leurs « droits politiques et civils ».

Khrushchev's successor, Leonid Brezhnev, meets Alexander Dubček of Czechoslovakia at the Bratislava summit, 7 August 1968. Two weeks later, Soviet tanks were crushing the Prague experiment in 'liberalization'.

Auf dem Gipfeltreffen in Bratislava trifft Chruschtschows Amtsnachfolger Leonid Breschnew den Staatschef der Tschechoslowakei Alexander Dubček, 7. August 1968. Zwei Wochen später rollen sowjetische Panzer das Prager Experiment der „Liberalisierung" nieder.

Rencontre entre le successeur de Khrouchtchev, Leonid Brejnev, et le tchécoslovaque Alexandre Dubček lors du sommet de Bratislava, 7 août 1968. Deux semaines plus tard, les tanks soviétiques réprimaient la tentative pragoise de « libéralisation ».

March 1962. Gary
Powers, pilot of the
U2 spy plane that
crashed in the Soviet
Union, gives
evidence before a US
Senate Armed Forces
Committee,
Washington DC.

März 1962. Gary
Powers, der Pilot des
Aufklärungsflugzeugs
U2, das während
eines Spionageflugs
über der Sowjet-
union abstürzte, sagt
vor einem Militär-
ausschuß der ameri-
kanischen Streit-
kräfte in Washington
D.C. aus.

Mars 1962. Gary
Powers, le pilote de
l'avion d'espionnage
U2 qui s'était écrasé
en Union soviétique,
témoigne devant un
comité de l'armée de
l'air américaine au
Sénat, Washington
D.C.

The Cuban missiles on their way back to the Soviet Union. This picture was taken from a US reconnaissance aircraft, 12 November 1962. The missiles can be seen lashed to the deck of the cargo ship.

Kubanische Raketen auf ihrem Rückweg in die Sowjetunion. Dieses Foto wurde von einem amerikanischen Aufklärungsflugzeug aus aufgenommen, 12. November 1962. Die Raketen sind auf dem Deck des Schiffs stationiert.

Les missiles cubains réexpédiés en Union soviétique. Ce cliché fut pris par un avion de reconnaissance américain, 12 novembre 1962. On peut apercevoir les missiles, arrimés sur le pont du navire.

In the year of his election victory, John Kennedy relaxes in his rocking chair. It brought him relief from frequent back pain.

Im Jahr des Wahlsiegs gönnt sich der von Rückenbeschwerden geplagte John Kennedy eine Entspannungspause im Schaukelstuhl.

L'année de son élection victorieuse. John Kennedy se détend dans son rocking chair. Ce siège le soulageait de ses fréquents maux de dos.

Jacqueline Lee Bouvier, better known as Jackie Kennedy, 1961. She sometimes wearied of being one half of a couple known as 'Jack and Jackie'.

Jacqueline Lee Bouvier, besser bekannt als Jackie Kennedy, 1961. Sie fand ihre Rolle in dem berühmten Gespann „Jack und Jackie" nicht immer leicht.

Jacqueline Lee Bouvier, plus connue sous le nom de Jackie Kennedy, 1961. Elle était parfois lasse d'être la moitié de ce couple surnommé « Jack et Jackie ».

The shots that shook the world, Dallas,
22 November 1963. The JFK motorcade sweeps
past the grassy knoll and all hell breaks out.

Die Schüsse von Dallas erschütterten die Welt,
22. November 1963. Als die Wagenkolonne
JFKs an der Grasfläche vorbeifährt, treffen ihn
die tödlichen Kugeln.

Les coups de feu qui ébranlèrent le monde,
Dallas, 22 novembre 1963. Le cortège de JFK
passe devant ce monticule d'herbe, puis c'est le
cauchemar.

Officially, this is the rifle with which Lee Harvey Oswald shot President Kennedy. The picture was taken in 1965, during the Warren Commission inquiry into the assassination.

Offiziell ist dies das Gewehr, mit dem Lee Harvey Oswald Präsident Kennedy erschoß. Die Aufnahme stammt aus dem Jahre 1965, als die Warren-Kommission versuchte, den Fall aufzuklären.

Officiellement, ce fusil est celui qu'utilisa Lee Harvey Oswald pour abattre le président Kennedy. Ce cliché fut pris en 1965, au cours de l'enquête menée par la commission Warren sur l'assassinat.

Ninety-nine minutes after the shots were fired, Lyndon Johnson is sworn
in as president of the United States on board *Air Force One*, 22
November 1963. On his right is Mrs Johnson, on his left, Jackie Kennedy.

Neunundneunzig Minuten nach dem Attentat wurde Lyndon Johnson
als neuer Präsident der Vereinigten Staaten an Bord der *Air Force One*
vereidigt, 22. November 1963. Rechts neben ihm steht Mrs Johnson,
links von ihm Jackie Kennedy.

Quatre-vingt-dix-neuf minutes après que les coups de feu aient été tirés,
Lyndon Johnson, nommé président des Etats-Unis, prête serment à bord
de l'avion *Air Force One*, 22 novembre 1963. À sa droite, Mme Johnson,
et à sa gauche, Jackie Kennedy.

Jack Ruby kills Lee Harvey Oswald, 24 November 1963. The incident happened as Oswald was being led out of the basement of the Dallas municipal office, and was seen by millions on television.

Jack Ruby erschießt Lee Harvey Oswald, 24. November 1963. Der Vorfall ereignete sich, als Oswald aus dem Untergeschoß der Polizeibehörde von Dallas hinausgeführt wurde, und wurde von Millionen am Fernseher verfolgt.

Jack Ruby tua Lee Harvey Oswald, 24 novembre 1963. L'incident se produisit alors qu'Oswald sortait du sous-sol du tribunal de Dallas. Des millions de téléspectateurs assistèrent à la scène.

Ernesto Che
Guevara, Argentinian
revolutionary leader,
1965. Guevara
helped Fidel Castro
in his war to free
Cuba. In the Sixties,
his picture became
an icon for the Left.

Ernesto Che
Guevara, argentini-
scher Revolutions-
führer, 1965. Er
unterstützte Fidel
Castro in seinem
Kampf um die Be-
freiung Kubas. Sein
Bild wurde in den
sechziger Jahren für
die Linken zur Ikone.

Ernesto Che
Guevara, le leader
révolutionnaire
argentin, 1965.
Guevara combattit
aux côtés de Fidel
Castro pour libérer
Cuba. Cette photo-
graphie devint une
icône pour la gauche
dans les années
soixante.

January 1962.
Prime Minister Fidel
Castro 'at bat' to
open a baseball
tournament in
Havana, Cuba.

Januar 1962.
Premierminister
Fidel Castro, am
Schlagholz, eröffnet
ein Baseball-Turnier
in Havanna, Kuba.

Janvier 1962.
Coup d'envoi d'un
tournoi de base-ball
donné par le Premier
ministre Fidel Castro
à La Havane, Cuba.

Mao Zedong relaxes, 1963. His popularity in China waned in the early
Sixties, after the comparative failure of the 'Great Leap Forward'. Three years
later came the Cultural Revolution, and Mao was once more in firm control.

Mao Tse-tung entspannt sich, 1963. Nachdem sein politisches Programm
des „Großen Sprungs nach vorn" Anfang der sechziger Jahre scheiterte,
hatte er an Popularität verloren. Drei Jahre später gewann Mao während
der Kulturrevolution wieder die politische Oberhand im Staat.

Repos pour Mao Tsé-toung, 1963. Sa popularité en Chine déclina au début
des années soixante après le relatif échec du « Grand Bond en avant ».
Trois ans plus tard, Mao lançait la Révolution culturelle et réaffirmait une
fois de plus son pouvoir.

A chorus sing the praises of their beloved Mao during a break
in the wheat harvest near Beijing, July 1967. No doubt *The
Thoughts of Chairman Mao* were in the thoughts of every singer.

Der Chor singt ein Loblied auf den großen Kommunistenführer
Mao während einer Pause bei der Weizenernte in der Nähe von
Beijing, Juli 1967. Kein Zweifel *Die Gedanken des Kommu-
nistenführers Mao* beherrschten die Gedanken jedes Sängers.

Un choeur chante les louanges du vénéré Mao lors d'une pause
durant la récolte de blé près de Pékin, juillet 1967. Il va sans
dire que chaque chanteur avait en tête *Les pensées du président
Mao*.

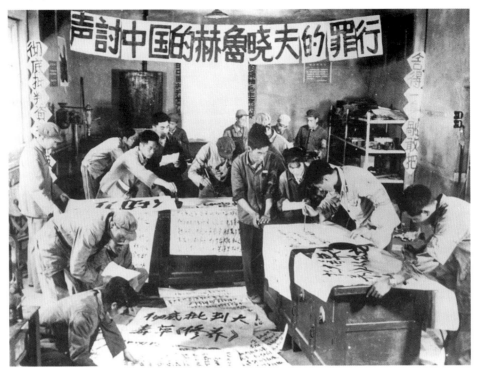

October 1967, and the Chinese Cultural Revolution is well under way. Members of
the Provincial Revolution Committee paint anti-capitalist slogans on banners, as part
of a drive to attack those in authority deemed to have capitalist leanings.

Oktober 1967, die Chinesische Kulturrevolution läuft auf Hochtouren. Mitglieder
des Revolutionskomitees bemalen Fahnen mit antikapitalistischen Parolen. Sie klagen
jene alten Kräfte in China an, die ihre kapitalistischen Pfründe sichern wollen.

Octobre 1967, en pleine Révolution culturelle chinoise. Les membres d'un comité
révolutionnaire de province peignent des slogans anticapitalistes sur des bannières
lors d'une campagne menée contre certains dirigeants tentés par le capitalisme.

Holding copies
of the famous
Little Red Book,
followers of Mao
taunt members of
the Chinese embassy
staff in London,
1967.

Eine Ausgabe des
berühmten *Kleinen
Roten Buchs* in der
Hand, verhöhnen
Anhänger Maos Mit-
glieder der chinesi-
schen Botschaft in
London, 1967.

Le célèbre *Petit Livre
rouge* en main, des
partisans de Mao
persiflent le person-
nel de l'ambassade
de Chine à Londres,
1967.

Political campaigning, US style. Holding placards that read 'I like Dick' and 'Hump for Crump', Republican supporters from the Clothing Export Council back their nomination, Nixon, and show their opposition to Humphrey, in the 1968 presidential election.

Wahlkampf im amerikanischen Stil. Im Präsidentschaftswahlkampf von 1968 unterstützt der Rat für den Bekleidungsexport den republikanischen Kandidaten Nixon mit Plakaten, die Aufschriften haben wie „I like Dick" und „Hump for Crump". Dabei zeigen sie auch ihre Ablehnung gegenüber Humphrey.

Campagne à l'américaine durant les élections présidentielles de 1968. Munies de pancartes « J'aime Dick » et « A bas Hump », ces membres du Conseil pour l'exportation de l'habillement affichent leur soutien à Nixon, le candidat républicain, et leur hostilité à Humphrey.

On the trail to the White House, November 1968. Richard Milhous Nixon looks unnaturally confident in his bid to become president – Nixon's return to power was a close call.

Auf dem Weg ins Weiße Haus, November 1968. Richard Milhous Nixon scheint sich seiner Sache sicher zu sein, der nächste Präsident zu werden – Nixons Wahlsieg war knapp.

Sur la route de la Maison Blanche, novembre 1968. Richard Milhous Nixon semble étonnamment sûr de lui durant la campagne présidentielle – Nixon fut ramené au pouvoir de justesse.

New Delhi, April 1961. The Dalai Lama (left), leader of Tibet, meets Jawaharlal Nehru, prime minister of India. They were discussing the rehabilitation of Tibetans who had crossed the Indian border during the Sino-Tibetan crisis.

Neu-Delhi, April 1961. Der Dalai Lama (links), religiöses Oberhaupt von Tibet, trifft den indischen Premierminister Jawaharlal Nehru. Anlaß des Treffens war die Rehabilitierung von Tibetern, die während der Sino-Tibet-Krise nach Indien geflohen waren.

New Delhi, avril 1961. Rencontre entre le dalaï-lama (à gauche), le représentant du Tibet, et Jawaharlal Nehru, le Premier ministre indien, pour discuter de l'intégration des Tibétains réfugiés en Inde pendant la crise sino-tibétaine.

Members of the Gandhi dynasty of India, in the garden of their New Delhi home, 1967. (Left to right) Sanjay Gandhi, his mother Indira Gandhi (then prime minister of India), and his brother Rajiv.

Mitglieder der Gandhi-Dynastie in Indien im Garten ihres Hauses in Neu-Delhi, 1967. (Von links nach rechts) Sanjay Gandhi, seine Mutter Indira Gandhi (damals Premierminister von Indien) und sein Bruder Rajiv.

Les membres de la dynastie des Ghandi dans le jardin de leur demeure à New Delhi, Inde, 1967. (De gauche à droite), Sanjay Gandhi, sa mère Indira Gandhi (alors Premier ministre de l'Inde) et son frère Rajiv.

A brief happy moment in a year which was largely spent on the run from the authorities. Winnie and Nelson Mandela embrace, 1962.

Ein kurzer Augenblick des Glücks in einem Jahr, in dem sie ansonsten zum größten Teil auf der Flucht vor den Behörden waren. Winnie und Nelson Mandela umarmen einander, 1962.

Bref instant de bonheur au cours d'une année essentiellement dominée par la nécessité de fuir les autorités. Winnie dans les bras de Nelson Mandela, 1962.

Eminence Blanche: Dr Hendrik Verwoerd, prime minister of South Africa and high priest of the foul doctrine of apartheid, March 1961.

Weiße Eminenz: Dr. Hendrik Verwoerd, Premierminister von Südafrika und scharfer Verfechter der rassendiskriminierenden Apartheidpolitik, März 1961.

L'éminence blanche : le Dr. Hendrik Verwoerd, Premier ministre de l'Afrique du Sud et fervent défenseur de l'immonde doctrine de l'apartheid, mars 1961.

August 1966. Charles de Gaulle, president of the French Fifth Republic, mingles with crowds in Addis Abeba, Ethiopia, during his world tour. He had just visited the Liberation Memorial, where he received a better reception than he would have been given in Algeria.

August 1966. Staatspräsident der Fünften Französischen Republik Charles de Gaulle mischt sich unter das Volk in Addis Abeba, Äthiopien, während seiner Weltreise. Gerade hatte er die Gedenkstätte des Befreiungskampfes besucht, wo man ihn freundlicher empfangen hatte, als dies in Algerien der Fall gewesen war.

Août 1966. Charles de Gaulle, président de la Vᵉ République, mêlé à la foule à Addis Abeba, Ethiopie, lors de son voyage autour du monde. Il venait de se rendre au Mémorial de la libération où il fut mieux accueilli qu'en Algérie.

Harold Wilson, British prime minister, 1968. Wilson, too, had
his African problems. In November 1965, Ian Smith unilaterally
declared Rhodesia (now Zimbabwe) an independent state.

Harold Wilson, britischer Premierminister, 1968. Auch Wilson
sah sich in Afrika mit Problemen konfrontiert. Ian Smith
hatte Rhodesien (das heutige Simbabwe) im November 1965
mit politisch einseitiger Wirksamkeit für unabhängig erklärt.

Harold Wilson, Premier ministre britannique, 1968. Wilson
avait lui aussi sa part de problèmes africains. En novembre
1965, Ian Smith déclara unilatéralement l'indépendance de
la Rhodésie (aujourd'hui le Zimbabwe).

2. Conflict
Konflikte
Conflits

One of the many haunting images from the bloodiest war of the decade. A US infantryman carries a wounded refugee from the carnage of Vietnam, 25 October 1968. It was the year in which millions of Americans, appalled by what they had seen on television, began to doubt that the United States would win.

Eins der vielen unvergeßlichen Bilder der blutigsten Auseinandersetzung des Jahrzehnts. Ein US-Soldat trägt einen verwundeten Flüchtling aus dem Kampfgebiet in Vietnam, 25. Oktober 1968. Es war das Jahr, in welchem Millionen von Amerikanern, entsetzt von dem, was sie auf den Bildschirmen verfolgten, schließlich am Sieg der Vereinigten Staaten zu zweifeln begannen.

Une des nombreuses images obsédantes de la guerre la plus sanglante de la décennie. Un soldat américain emmène une réfugiée blessée loin du carnage de la guerre du Viêt-nam, 25 octobre 1968. Ce fut cette année-là que des millions d'Américains, horrifiés par les images diffusées à la télévision, commencèrent à douter de la victoire des Etats-Unis.

2. Conflict
Konflikte
Conflits

The world had at last recovered from World War II. Europe and Japan had been rebuilt. The cars, luxury goods, food and money that had been in short supply in the immediate post-war years of the Forties and Fifties were now flooding the markets. It was time for new conflicts.

The Sixties were the years when everyone took sides – when, for a while, everyone lived in everyone else's backyard. It didn't matter where the riots, wars and revolutions were raging. It didn't matter who you were – Khrushchev, Kennedy or a complete unknown. What mattered was how each struggle was resolved. Many believed they were living through the opening salvoes of the final showdown between Capitalism and Communism, freedom and totalitarianism.

Much of Europe teetered on the brink of revolution. Most of southern Africa was on the brink of a bloodbath. Within a few years, the stability of France was threatened first by the extreme Right, and then by the extreme Left. The struggle for independence tore Algeria, Kenya, Cyprus, Aden and Nigeria apart.

By the time the dust settled in Sharpeville, My Lai, Prague, the Golan Heights, Nicosia, Leopoldville and the Bay of Pigs, a new and frightened world had been created.

Die Welt hatte sich gerade von den Folgen des Zweiten Weltkrieges erholt. Der Wiederaufbau von Europa und Japan war abgeschlossen. Autos, Luxusgüter, Lebensmittel und Geld, alles, was während der Nachkriegsjahre in den vierziger und fünfziger Jahren knapp war, überflutete nun die Märkte. Es war die Zeit für neue Konflikte.

Die sechziger Jahre waren ein Jahrzehnt, in dem jedermann Stellung bezog, und in dem sich für eine kurze Zeit, jeder in die Angelegenheiten des anderen einmischte. Es spielte dabei keine Rolle, wo die Unruhen, Kriege und Revolutionen tobten. Es spielte auch keine Rolle, wer man war – ob Chruschtschow, Kennedy oder jemand völlig unbekanntes. Was zählte war, wie jeder Konflikt zu lösen sei. Viele glaubten, den entscheidenden Kampf zwischen Kapitalismus und Kommunismus mitzuerleben, zwischen Freiheit und Totalitarismus.

Große Teile Europas befanden sich am Rande einer Revolution. Weite Teile Südafrikas drohten in einem Blutbad unterzugehen. Innerhalb weniger Jahre war die innere Stabilität Frankreichs zuerst durch die extreme Rechte, dann durch die Ultralinke bedroht. Der Kampf um Unabhängigkeit zerriss Algerien, Kenia, Zypern, Aden und Nigeria.

Als sich die Wogen in Sharpeville, My Lai, Prag, auf den Golanhöhen, in Nikosia, Leopoldville und in der Schweinebucht wieder geglättet hatten, war eine neue und erschreckende Welt geboren.

Le monde avait enfin pansé les plaies de la Seconde Guerre mondiale. La reconstruction de l'Europe et du Japon était accomplie. Les voitures, les produits de luxe, la nourriture et l'argent qui avaient tant fait défaut durant l'après-guerre et les années quarante et cinquante envahissaient désormais tous les marchés. L'heure avait sonné pour de nouveaux conflits.

Les années soixante furent les temps pendant lesquels tout le monde prit position et durant lesquels, pendant un court laps de temps, tout le monde sembla à l'écoute de l'autre. Peu importe où les émeutes, les guerres et les révolutions faisaient rage. Peu importe que les acteurs soient Khrouchtchev, Kennedy ou un illustre inconnu. Ce qui importait était la manière dont chaque conflit sérait résolu. Nombreux étaient ceux qui pensaient vivre une époque témoin des derniers soubresauts de l'ultime lutte entre capitalisme et communisme, entre liberté et totalitarisme.

Une grande partie de l'Europe était au bord de la révolution. Presque tous les pays du sud de l'Afrique étaient sur le point de vivre un carnage. En l'espace de quelques années, la stabilité de la France se trouva menacée par l'extrême-droite, puis par l'extrême-gauche. La lutte pour l'indépendance déchira l'Algérie, le Kenya, Chypre, Aden au Yémen et le Nigeria.

Quand le calme revint enfin à Sharpeville, à My Lai, à Prague, sur les collines du Golan, à Nicosie, à Léopoldville et dans la baie des Cochons, un monde nouveau et effrayant était né.

Palestine refugees cross the Allenby Bridge over the River Jordan during the Six-Day War, June 1967. The bridge had been blown up to hinder pursuit by Israeli troops but, in a series of lightning attacks, the Israelis gained control of the West Bank.

Palästinensische Flüchtlinge überqueren den Jordan über die Allenby-Brücke während des Sechstagekrieges, Juni 1967. Die Brücke war gesprengt worden, um das Vorrücken der israelischen Truppen zu stoppen, doch mit einer Reihe von Blitzangriffen erlangten die Israeli die Kontrolle über die West Bank zurück.

Réfugiés palestiniens traversant le pont Allenby sur la rivière du Jourdain durant, la guerre des Six Jours, juin 1967. Le pont avait été détruit pour freiner l'avancée des troupes israéliennes. Mais, suite à une série d'attaques éclair, les Israéliens parvinrent à prendre le contrôle de la rive ouest.

An Israeli soldier studies a burning oil refinery on the Egyptian side of the Suez Canal, June 1967. 'We are making mincemeat of everything on the ground,' reported Mordechai Hod, an Israeli Air Force commander.

Ein israelischer Soldat beobachtet eine brennende Ölraffinerie auf der ägyptischen Seite des Suezkanals, Juni 1967. „Wir machen Hackfleisch aus allem, was sich bewegt", berichtete der israelische Luftwaffenkommandant Mordechai Hod.

Un soldat israélien observe une raffinerie de pétrole en feu du côté égyptien du canal de Suez, juin 1967. « On fait de la chair à pâté de tout ce qu'il y a au sol » déclara Mordechai Hod, un commandant de l'armée de l'air israélienne.

Israeli forces with a convoy of Egyptian prisoners during the Six-Day War. The Egyptian army and air force were both humiliated during the war, and Nasser sought to resign as president of the United Arab Republic.

Israelische Truppen mit einem Konvoi ägyptischer Kriegsgefangener während des Sechstagekrieges. Die ägyptische Armee und Luftwaffe erlitten während dieses Krieges eine Niederlage, und Nasser ersuchte um seinen Rücktritt als Präsident der Vereinigten Arabischen Republik.

Soldats israéliens escortant un convoi de prisonniers égyptiens durant la guerre des Six Jours. Les armées de terre et de l'air égyptiennes furent humiliées au cours de cette guerre et Nasser voulut démissionner de son poste de président de la République arabe unie.

The same city, the same park, the same grass and trees
– but two different benches. Salisbury, Rhodesia, during
the days of 'separate development', 1967.

Dieselbe Stadt, derselbe Park, dasselbe Gras und
dieselben Bäume – jedoch zwei verschiedene Bänke.
Salisbury, Rhodesien, in der Zeit der „getrennten
Entwicklung", 1967.

La même ville, le même parc, la même herbe, les mêmes
arbres – mais deux bancs différents. Salisbury, Rhodésie,
à l'époque du « développement séparé », 1967.

The infamous Pass
Laws in operation in
South Africa, April
1960. All black
citizens had to
produce identity
passes on demand.

Durchführung der
menschenverachten-
den Paßgesetze, Süd-
afrika, April 1960.
Jeder schwarze Bür-
ger mußte auf Ver-
langen seinen Paß
vorzeigen.

Application des
infâmes lois de
contrôle d'identité
en Afrique du Sud,
avril 1960. Les
citoyens noirs étaient
obligés de présenter
une pièce d'identité
en cas de contrôle.

21 March 1960. In
Sharpeville, South
African police open
fire on unarmed
protestors, killing 67
and wounding 186.

21. März 1960. In
Sharpeville eröffnen
Polizeitruppen das
Feuer auf unbewaff-
nete Demonstranten,
67 wurden getötet
und 186 verletzt.

21 mars 1960. A
Sharpeville, la police
sud-africaine ouvrit
le feu sur des
manifestants non
armés, 67 morts et
186 blessés.

The *Rhodesia Herald* proudly proclaims Rhodesia's unilateral Declaration
of Independence, November 1965. The Prime Minister Ian Smith promised
that there would be permanent white minority rule. It lasted just 11 years.

Der *Rhodesia Herald* verkündet stolz die einseitige Unabhängigkeitserklärung Rhodesiens, November 1965. Premierminister Ian Smith versicherte, es
gebe weiterhin eine weiße Minderheitsregierung. Sein Versprechen hielt nur
11 Jahre.

Le *Rhodesia Herald* annonce fièrement la Déclaration d'indépendance
unilatérale de la Rhodésie, novembre 1965. Le Premier ministre, Ian Smith,
promit qu'il y aurait toujours une minorité blanche au sein du gouvernement. Elle ne dura que 11 ans.

November 1965. Ian Smith walks by Victoria Falls on his first public appearance after the Declaration of Independence. 'I don't believe in black majority rule in Rhodesia…,' he said, '…not in a thousand years.'

November 1965. Ian Smith spaziert bei seinem ersten öffentlichen Auftritt nach der Unabhängigkeitserklärung an den Viktoria-Wasserfällen. „Ich glaube nicht an eine schwarze Mehrheitsregierung in Rhodesien…", sagte er, „nicht in tausend Jahren."

Novembre 1965. Première sortie publique d'Ian Smith près des chutes de Victoria après la Déclaration d'indépendance. « Je ne crois pas en un gouvernement à majorité noire en Rhodésie … », déclara-t-il, « … même dans mille ans ».

April 1967. Still policing the British Empire. A Northumberland Fusilier heavy-handedly imposes law and order in Aden,
which had been the first imperial acquisition in Queen
Victoria's reign.

April 1967. Noch wird das Britische Empire kontrolliert. Ein
schwerbewaffneter Infanterist sorgt in Aden, der ersten Kron-
kolonie unter Königin Viktorias Regentschaft brutal für Ruhe
und Ordnung.

Avril 1967. L'Empire britannique toujours régenté. Un fusilier
de Northumberland fait brutalement la loi à Aden, première
conquête impériale datant de l'ère victorienne.

An Aden civilian crouches in terror as British soldiers threaten him during nationalist demonstrations. The British withdrawal, when it finally came, was a masterly piece of organization.

Ein Adener Zivilist kauert verängstigt am Boden als ihn englische Soldaten während nationalistischer Demonstrationen bedrohen. Der britische Rückzug war, als er endlich kam, ein Meisterstück der Organisation.

Pendant les manifestations nationalistes, un habitant d'Aden terrorisé ne bouge plus sous la menace de ces soldats britanniques. Le retrait britannique, quand il eut enfin lieu, fut magistralement orchestré.

A French soldier
patrols the Casbah,
Algiers, during the
war of Algerian
Independence, 1962.

Ein französischer
Soldat während des
algerischen Unab-
hängigkeitskrieges
patrouilliert in der
Kasbah Algiers,
1962.

Un soldat français
en patrouille dans
la Casbah, Alger,
durant la guerre
d'Algérie, 1962.

The same Casbah in
the uneasy days that
followed de Gaulle's
ceasefire agreement
with the National
Liberation Front
(FLN), March 1962.

In derselben Kasbah,
die den schwierigen
Tagen des Waffen-
stillstandsabkom-
mens de Gaulles mit
der Nationalen Be-
freiungsfront (FLN),
folgten, März 1962.

La Casbah durant
une période difficile,
celle qui suivit l'ac-
cord d'un cessez-le-
feu entre de Gaulle
et le Front de libé-
ration nationale
(FLN), mars 1962.

July 1968. A Federal soldier swings a grenade by its release pin as he guards
Ibo women and children prisoners during the Biafran War. The war lasted two
and a half years, and a million innocent people died of starvation.

Juli 1968. Ein Bundessoldat bewacht gefangene Frauen und Kinder des Ibo-
Stammes und schwingt dabei bedrohlich eine Handgranate, die er am Auslöser
hält. Der Krieg in Biafra dauerte zweieinhalb Jahre, dabei starben eine Million
unschuldiger Menschen an den Folgen von Unterernährung.

Juillet 1968. Un soldat français joue avec la goupille d'une grenade tout en
surveillant des femmes et des enfants Ibo faits prisonniers durant la guerre
du Biafra. Cette guerre dura deux ans et demi et un million d'innocents
moururent de faim.

Jomo Kenyatta (left) and the Mau Mau leader Field-Marshal Mwariama, 1961.
Kenyatta led the independence movement for Kenya, and became its first prime minister.
The picture was taken shortly after his release from nine years' imprisonment.

Jomo Kenyatta (links) und der Mau-Mau-Anführer Feldmarschall Mwariama, 1961.
Kenyatta war Anführer der Unabhängigkeitsbewegung in Kenia und wurde der erste
Premierminister des Landes. Diese Aufnahme entstand kurz nach seiner Freilassung nach
neun Jahren Haft.

Jomo Kenyatta (à gauche) et le chef des Mau-Mau, le maréchal Mwariama, 1961.
Kenyatta, qui dirigea le mouvement pour l'indépendance du Kenya, devint le Premier
ministre du pays. Ce cliché fut pris peu de temps après sa sortie de prison où il avait
passé neuf ans.

Don McCullin's photographs from troubled Cyprus. Greek Cypriots, armed with shotguns and primitive British Sten guns, patrol the streets, Nicosia, 1964. The struggle between the Greeks and Turks for control of the island has yet to be resolved.

Don McCullins Aufnahmen vom umkämpften Zypern. Griechische Zyprioten haben sich mit Schrotflinten und einfachen englischen Maschinengewehren bewaffnet, um die Straßen zu kontrollieren, Nikosia, 1964. Der Konflikt zwischen den Griechen und Türken, die um die Vormachtstellung auf der Insel kämpfen, ist bis zum heutigen Tag ungelöst.

Clichés pris par Don McCullin d'une Chypre tourmentée. Des Chypriotes grecs, armés de fusils et de vieux Sten britanniques, patrouillent dans les rues, Nicosie, 1964. Le conflit pour le contrôle de l'île opposant Grecs et Turcs n'était toujours pas résolu.

Limassol, Cyprus, 1964. Mourners cover a casualty in the civil war in Cyprus with the Turkish flag.

Limassol, Zypern, 1964. Trauernde bedecken ein Opfer des Bürgerkrieges mit der türkischen Flagge.

Limassol, Chypre, 1964. Les parents d'une victime de la guerre civile chypriote recouvrent son corps du drapeau turc.

Cypriot widows, victims of the civil war, 1964. A grieving woman
(above), whose husband has been killed in the fighting, is comforted by
friends. A neighbour (right) brings water to a widow and her child.

Zypriotische Witwen, Opfer des Bürgerkrieges, 1964. Eine trauernde Frau
(oben), deren Mann während der Kämpfe getötet wurde, wird von Freunden
getröstet. Eine Nachbarin (rechts) bringt einer Witwe und deren Kind Wasser.

Veuves chypriotes, victimes de la guerre civile, 1964. Une femme en pleurs
(ci-dessus) dont le mari a été tué au combat est réconfortée par des proches.
Une voisine (à droite) apporte de l'eau à une veuve et son enfant.

Czechoslovakia, August 1968. Hope and terror as the Prague Spring
nears its end. The picture was taken shortly after the Soviet invasion
with troops from Poland, Hungary, Bulgaria and East Germany.

Tschechoslowakei, August 1968. Hoffnung und Terror zum Ende
des Prager Frühlings. Diese Aufnahme entstand kurz nach dem
sowjetischen Einmarsch mit Truppen aus Polen, Ungarn, Bulgarien
und der DDR.

Tchécoslovaquie, août 1968. Espoir et terreur alors que le
« printemps de Prague » touche à sa fin. Ce cliché fut pris juste
après l'invasion soviétique menée avec des soldats polonais,
hongrois, bulgares et est-allemands.

A Soviet tank rolls along the streets of Prague. The Czechs had sought to soften and reform their communist government in a 'socialist democratic revolution'. About 670,000 troops were sent to occupy their country.

Ein sowjetischer Panzer rollt durch die Straßen Prags. Die Tschechen hatten versucht, ihre kommunistische Regierung mit der „sozialistisch-demokratischen Revolution" zu reformieren. Mehr als 670.000 Soldaten wurden geschickt, um ihr Land zu besetzen.

Un char soviétique circulant dans les rues de Prague. Les Tchèques avaient tenté d'assouplir et de réformer leur gouvernement communiste en menant une « révolution socialiste démocratique ». Plus de 670 000 soldats furent envoyés pour occuper leur pays.

16 April 1961. Castro's victorious soldiers at (above) the Playa de Citron, and (right) the Playa de Giron, Cuba, after successfully repelling the US backed invasion at the Bay of Pigs. It was a humiliating defeat for the CIA, who had planned and controlled the operation.

16. April 1961. Castros siegreichen Soldaten an der Playa de Citron (oben) und an der Playa de Giron (rechts), Kuba, gelang es, die amerikanische Invasion in der Schweinebucht zu verhindern. Es war eine schwere Niederlage für die CIA, die die Operation geplant und überwacht hatte.

16 avril 1961. Des soldats de Castro victorieux à la Playa de Citron (ci-dessus) et sur la Playa de Girón, (à droite) Cuba, où ils réussirent à repousser l'invasion de la baie des Cochons, soutenue par les États-Unis. Ce fut une défaite humiliante pour la CIA qui avait préparé et mené l'opération.

The war in Vietnam escalates, 1965. The flash from a triple salvo of guns on the USS *Canberra*
lights up the night sky as they shell the North Vietnamese coast. The previous year the USA had
been acting in a purely 'advisory' capacity – with 23,000 troops in South Vietnam.

Der Krieg in Vietnam eskaliert, 1965. Das Leuchtfeuer aus den dreigeschossigen Kanonen der USS
Canberra erhellt den Nachthimmel vor der nordvietnamesischen Küste. Noch im Jahr zuvor hatten
die Amerikaner eine rein „beratende" Funktion – mit 23.000 in Südvietnam stationierten Soldaten.

Intensification de la guerre au Viêt-nam, 1965. La nuit illuminée par une triple décharge d'obus
tirée du navire américain USS *Canberra* sur la côte nord du Viêt-nam. L'année précédente, les Etats-
Unis avait agi en tant que simples « conseillers », avec 23 000 soldats basés au Viêt-nam du Sud.

June 1967. An American 175mm projectile blasts from a gun at Camp Carroll in the Qang Tri province, Vietnam.

Juni 1967. US-Soldaten feuern ein 175-mm-Geschoß von Camp Carroll aus in die Provinz Qang Tri ab, Vietnam.

Juin 1967. Un projectile américain de 175 mm tiré d'un canon installé à Camp Carroll dans la province de Qang Tri, Viêt-nam.

April 1968. US soldiers take cover in a Vietnam trench
near Hill Timothy. This picture is one of a famous set
of photographs taken by Terry Fincher.

April 1968. US-Soldaten suchen Schutz in einem viet-
namesischen Schützengraben in der Nähe von Hill
Timothy. Diese Aufnahme gehört zu einer berühmten
Serie von Fotos, die Terry Fincher aufnahm.

Avril 1968. Des soldats américains à l'abri dans une
tranchée près de Hill Timothy, Viêt-nam. Ce cliché fait
partie d'une célèbre série de photographies prises par
Terry Fincher.

April 1969.
Members of the
Vietnam National
Liberation Front
(Vietcong) fire a
machine gun at US
aircraft during a raid
in South Vietnam.

April 1969. Mitglie-
der der Nationalen
Befreiungsfront Viet-
nams (Vietcong)
feuern mit einem
Maschinengewehr
auf ein US-Flugzeug
während eines Luft-
angriffes auf Süd-
vietnam.

Avril 1969. Des
soldats du Front de
libération nationale
du Viêt-nam (les
Viêt-cong) tirant sur
un avion américain
lors d'un raid au
Viêt-nam du Sud.

Wounded American soldiers on Hill Timothy, April 1968. Two months earlier, President Johnson had declared at a Washington press conference that the Vietnam Tet offensive was a 'complete failure'.

Verwundete amerikanische Soldaten auf Hill Timothy, April 1968. US-Präsident Johnson hatte zwei Monate zuvor auf einer Pressekonferenz in Washington erklärt, daß die Tet-Offensive ein „kompletter Fehlschlag" gewesen sei.

Soldats américains blessés à Timothy Hill, avril 1968. Deux mois plus tôt, le président Johnson avait déclaré lors d'une conférence de presse à Washington que l'offensive du Têt avait été un « échec complet ».

October 1968. Terry Fincher's study of military irony as a skull keeps watch over US soldiers in a Vietnamese jungle camp.

Oktober 1968. Terry Fincher dokumentiert den makaberen Humor der Militärs. Ein Totenschädel hält über US-Soldaten Wache in einem vietnamesischem Dschungellager.

Octobre 1968. L'ironie militaire vue par Terry Fincher. Une tête de mort pour faire le guet d'un camp de soldats américains dans la jungle vietnamienne.

US troops leap from Sikorsky S-55 helicopters into a swampy field, Vietnam, March 1966. The action was part of a raid to clean out a Vietcong position. The white smoke is from a phosphorous rocket used as a landing marker by a *Bird Dog* observation plane.

US-Soldaten springen von Militärhubschraubern der Marke Sikorsky S-55 über einem Sumpfgebiet ab, Vietnam, März 1966. Diese Aktion war Teil eines Angriffes, um Vietcong-Stellungen zu zerstören. Der weiße Rauch stammt von einer Phosphorrakete, die ein Aufklärungsflugzeug, *Bird Dog*, zur Landemarkierung abfeuerte.

Soldats américains débarquant des helicoptères S-55 Sikorsky dans un champ marécageux, Viêt-nam, mars 1966. Ce fut au cours d'un raid mené pour nettoyer une position viêt-cong. La fumée blanche provient d'une fusée phosphoreuse tirée d'un avion de reconnaissance *Bird Dog* pour marquer le terrain d'aterrissage.

February 1968. A US Marine weeps in
Vietnam, as a helicopter brings back survivors
from yet another bloody engagement.

Februar 1968. Einem US-Marineinfanteristen
laufen in Vietnam die Tränen übers Gesicht,
als ihn ein Hubschrauber mit anderen Überlebenden von einem blutigen Einsatz zurück-
fliegt.

Février 1968. Un marine américain pleure
au Viêt-nam dans l'hélicoptère qui ramène les
survivants d'un raid meurtrier, un de plus.

An American soldier drags a frightened man from a hiding place, 1965. The man could have been spy, enemy soldier or innocent civilian. Photographed by Don McCullin.

Ein amerikanischer Soldat zerrt einen verängstigten Vietnamesen aus seinem Versteck, 1965. Der Mann hätte ein Spion, ein feindlicher Soldat oder ein unschuldiger Zivilist sein können. Diese Aufnahme stammt von Don McCullin.

Un soldat américain tire un homme apeuré hors de sa cachette, 1965. Cet homme pouvait aussi bien être un espion, un ennemi qu'un civil innocent. Cliché de Don McCullin.

Crossing a river in the Nghia Hung province, Vietnam, 1967. The US soldier is pushing his combat gear ahead of him on a raft. It was the simplest way to cross the river, but provided little cover from enemy fire.

Überquerung eines Flusses in der Provinz Nghia Hung, Vietnam, 1967. Der amerikanische Soldat hat seine Kampfausrüstung auf ein Floß gepackt, das er vor sich her treibt. Es war die einfachste Möglichkeit, einen Fluß zu durchqueren, bot aber wenig Schutz vor feindlichen Angriffen.

Traversée d'une rivière dans la province du Nghia Hung, Viêt-nam, 1967. Ce soldat américain pousse devant lui le radeau qui transporte sa tenue de combat. Ce mode de déplacement, le plus simple pour traverser la rivière, n'offrait guère de protection contre les tirs ennemis.

Vietnamese refugees crossing the Perfume River, February 1968.
The bridge had been destroyed by the military. Terry Fincher's picture
is a classic study of one of the saddest scenes from almost any war.

Vietnamesische Flüchtlinge überqueren den Fluß Perfume, Februar
1968. Die Brücke wurde von den Militärs zerstört. Terry Finchers
Aufnahme ist ein typisches Bild einer der traurigsten Szenen, die sich
in jedem Krieg abspielt.

Réfugiés vietnamiens traversant la rivière Parfum, février 1968.
Le pont avait été détruit par l'armée. Terry Fincher traite de manière
classique une scène de guerre des plus tristes et qui pourrait être
l'illustration de n'importe quel autre conflit.

3. Protest
Demonstrationen
Contestations

Martin Luther King, in Birmingham, Alabama, 1963. On 12 April, King and Dr Ralph Abernathy were arrested as they peacefully protested against the racism of Governor George Wallace's regime. Their arrest sparked off violence, and many were injured.

Martin Luther King in Birmingham, Alabama, 1963. Am 12. April wurden King und Dr. Ralph Abernathy verhaftet, weil sie gegen die Rassenpolitik von Gouverneur George Wallace gewaltlos demonstriert hatten. Ihre Inhaftierung löste eine Welle der Gewalt aus, und viele wurden verletzt.

Martin Luther King, à Birmingham, Alabama, 1963. Le 12 avril, King et Dr. Ralph Abernathy furent arrêtés alors qu'ils manifestaient sans violence contre la politique raciste du gouverneur George Wallace. Leur arrestation donna lieu à des émeutes qui firent de nombreux blessés.

3. Protest
Demonstrationen
Contestations

Whatever poets may say, the child is seldom 'politically' the father of the man. Many of those who spent their Swinging Sixties in flower-bedecked, drug-induced Nirvana later became waspishly intolerant of 'drop-outs'. Similarly, those who raged against authority on the streets of London, Paris, Washington DC, Johannesburg, Limassol, Berlin and a hundred other cities in that revolutionary decade, subsequently suffered changes of political heart and flocked to join their respective 'establishments'.

For a while it seemed the air was full of abuse and tear gas and paving slabs, the streets were alive with the sound of shattering glass, every wall was papered from top to bottom with the posters of exhortation, and every poster was splattered with blood.

But it wasn't all violence. The quiet unflinching dignity of the civil rights marchers in the United States wore down a system that had abused black people for nearly 200 years. In dozens of countries, protesters paraded their opposition to nuclear weapons with a stubbornness that had a half-life at least as long as the radioactivity they abhorred.

Meanwhile, in the wake of the Orange Day parades in July 1969, rioting broke out in many cities in Northern Ireland, and the Sixties began to set the agenda for the Seventies.

Was auch immer die Dichter sagen mögen, das Kind ist selten der „politische" Vater des Mannes. Viele der Blumenkinder aus den Swinging Sixties, die ihre Tage im Drogennebel verbrachten, wurden später „Aussteigern" gegenüber zu intoleranten Fanatikern. Auch jene, die in diesem revolutionären Jahrzehnt auf den Straßen von London, Paris, Washington D.C., Johannesburg, Limassol, Berlin und anderswo gegen die etablierten Strukturen demonstriert hatten, änderten nach und nach ihre politische Einstellung und kehrten schließlich in ihr bürgerliches Umfeld zurück, aus dem sie gekommen waren.

Zeitweise sah es so aus, als bestünde die Welt hauptsächlich aus Mißständen und Tränengas und durch die Luft fliegende Pflastersteine; die Straßen waren vom Lärm zersplitternder Fensterscheiben erfüllt; jede Mauer war von oben bis unten mit Plakaten beklebt, die revolutionäre Kampfparolen trugen, und jedes dieser Poster war mit Blut bespritzt.

Doch es herrschte nicht nur Gewalt. Die ebenso ruhigen wie beharrlichen Märsche der Bürgerrechtsbewegung in den Vereinigten Staaten, zwangen ein System in die Knie, das die Rechte der Schwarzen 200 Jahre lang mit Füßen getreten hatte. In dutzenden von Ländern demonstrierten die Menschen gegen Nuklearwaffen mit einer Bestimmtheit, die mindestens der Halbwertzeit von Radioaktivität gleichkam.

Inzwischen, nach den Märschen des Oranier-Ordens im Juli 1969, brachen vielerorts in Nordirland Unruhen aus, und die Sechziger gaben einen Vorgeschmack auf die siebziger Jahre.

Quoi qu'en disent les poètes, l'enfant est rarement le père « politique » de l'homme. Bon nombre de ceux qui vécurent leurs « swinging sixties » parés de fleurs et plongés dans le nirvana des drogues, devinrent par la suite farouchement sectaires à l'égard des marginaux. Quant à ceux qui, durant cette décennie révolutionnaire, étaient descendus dans les rues de Londres, Paris, Washington D.C., Johannesburg, Limassol, Berlin et de centaines d'autres villes pour protester contre le pouvoir établi, ils ne tardèrent pas à changer leur fusil d'épaule et à rejoindre les milieux bourgeois dont ils étaient issus.

Il y eut toute une période pendant laquelle on aurait dit que l'air était plein de gaz lacrymogène, d'abus et de pavés, que les rues résonnaient du bruit des vitrines brisées, que chaque mur était recouvert d'affiches incitant à la révolte et chaque affiche tachée de sang.

Mais tout n'était pas que violence. Aux Etats-Unis, la dignité calme et stoïque des manifestants du mouvement pour les droits civils permit de laminer un système qui avait exploité les Noirs pendant près de deux siècles. Dans des dizaines de pays, des manifestants défilaient pour protester contre les armes nucléaires avec une détermination qui semblait aussi indestructible que cette radioactivité tant détestée.

Enfin, après les défilés des orangistes de juillet 1969, des émeutes éclatèrent dans de nombreuses villes d'Irlande du Nord donnant déjà le ton des années soixante-dix.

The French tricolour flies high over crowds marching to the Arc de
Triomphe during the heady days of May 1968. At times up to
10,000 students fought the CRS riot police on the streets of Paris.

Die französische Trikolore fliegt hoch über den Massen, die an den
bewegten Tagen im Mai 1968 auf den Arc de Triomphe zumar-
schierten. Zeitweise bekämpften bis zu 10.000 Studenten die CRS
auf den Straßen von Paris.

Le drapeau tricolore français flotte sur la foule défilant en direction de l'Arc de Triomphe durant les jours agités de mai 1968.
Il est arrivé que 10 000 étudiants affrontent les CRS dans les rues
de Paris.

Daniel Cohn-Bendit, leader of the students' strike and more familiarly known as 'Danny the Red', addresses a street meeting at the Gare de l'Est, Paris, 14 May 1968.

Daniel Cohn-Bendit, Anführer des Studentenstreiks und besser bekannt als „Danny der Rote", hält eine Ansprache auf einem Treffen am Gare de l'Est, Paris, 14. Mai 1968.

Daniel Cohn-Bendit, leader de la grève des étudiants et plus connu sous le nom de « Danny le Rouge », fait un discours lors d'une assemblée dans la rue, gare de l'Est, Paris, 14 mai 1968.

'…But put your faith in tear gas…'
Though faced by overwhelming
opposition, a member of the Paris CRS
hurls a gas canister to disperse a section
of the crowd that had gathered on May
Day, 1968.

„ … Vertrau' dem Tränengas …"
Obwohl sich der Pariser Polizist einer
überwältigen Menschenmenge
gegenüber sah, schleuderte er einen
Tränengaskanister in die Massen, die
sich am 1. Mai versammelt hatten, um
sie dazu zu bewegen, sich aufzulösen.

« … Mais faites confiance au gaz
lacrymogène … » Bien que seul face à
une immense foule hostile, un CRS jette
une grenade de gaz lacrymogène pour
disperser une partie des manifestants,
1er mai 1968, Paris.

The fighting in Paris lasted for nearly four weeks. Buses and cars were overturned and set ablaze. 422 people were arrested. Over 600 were seriously injured. Here, a casualty is led away from one of the many battles.

Die Straßenschlachten von Paris hielten fast vier Wochen an. Busse und Autos wurden umgekippt und in Brand gesteckt. Es gab 422 Festnahmen und über 600 Schwerverletzte. Hier wird eine Verletzte von einem der zahlreichen Kampfplätze weggebracht.

Les émeutes parisiennes durèrent près de quatre semaines. Des bus et des voitures furent renversés et mis à feu. 422 personnes furent arrêtées. Il y eut plus de 600 blessés graves. Ici, une blessée est évacuée loin d'un des nombreux champs de bataille.

Paris, 7 May 1968. Some of the worst fighting took place in the Latin Quarter. Students hurl paving stones at police in the Rue St Jacques. The police respond with yet more tear gas.

Paris, 7. Mai 1968. Im Quartier Latin fanden die heftigsten Kämpfe statt. In der Rue St. Jacques werfen Studenten mit Pflastersteinen auf Polizisten. Die Polizei antwortete mit immer größeren Mengen an Tränengas.

Paris, 7 mai 1968. Le Quartier latin fut le théâtre des échauffourées les plus violentes. Des étudiants jettent des pavés sur des policiers, rue Saint Jacques. La police riposte à coup de grenades lacrymogènes.

April 1968. American National Guardsmen patrol the smouldering streets of Washington DC in the riots that followed the murder of Martin Luther King.

April 1968. Die amerikanische Nationalgarde patrouilliert in den zerstörten Straßen in Washington D.C., nachdem es nach der Ermordung Martin Luther Kings zu Unruhen gekommen war.

Avril 1968. Des gardes nationaux américains patrouillent dans les rues dévastées de Washington D.C. après les émeutes qui éclatèrent suite à l'assassinat de Martin Luther King.

Police arrest an
injured rioter
during civil rights
disturbances in
Newark, New Jersey,
August 1964.

Ein Polizist verhaftet
einen verletzten
Aufständischen
während der Bürger-
rechtsaufstände in
Newark, New Jersey,
August 1964.

Arrestation d'un
manifestant blessé
durant les troubles
provoqués par la
campagne pour
les droits civils à
Newark, New Jersey,
août 1964.

Time out from rioting, USA, 1961. Although most blacks supported
Martin Luther King's non-violent methods, there were those who
agreed with Robert F Williams, who urged: 'We must fight back.'

Auszeit von den Kämpfen, USA, 1961. Viele Schwarze folgten Martin
Luther Kings gewaltfreien Methoden, andere schlossen sich Robert
F. Williams an, der dazu aufrief: „Wir müssen zurückschlagen."

Loin des émeutes, Etats-Unis, 1961. Même si la majorité des Noirs
soutenait les méthodes non-violentes de Martin Luther King, d'autres
en revanche soutenaient Robert F. Williams dont le slogan était :
« Nous devons rendre les coups ».

Beaufort, South
Carolina, May 1965.
Members of the
Ku Klux Klan take
the oath of loyalty to
white supremacy.

Beaufort, South
Carolina, Mai 1965.
Mitglieder des Ku-
Klux-Klan legen
gegenüber der
weißen Suprematie
den Treueeid ab.

Beaufort, Caroline
du Sud, mai 1965.
Des membres du
Ku Klux Klan font
le serment de fidélité
à la suprématie
blanche.

Four women cheer the first Martin Luther King-led civil rights march from Selma,
Alabama to the State Capital, Montgomery, March 1965. One of the leaders of the
movement, Bernard Lafayette, described the bravery of some of Selma's citizens:
'No matter how bad a place is, some people got courage.'

Vier Frauen applaudieren dem ersten Bürgerrechtsmarsch, der von Martin Luther King
von Selma, Alabama, zur Hauptstadt des Bundesstaates Montgomery, März 1965. Bernard
Lafayette, einer der Anführer der Bewegung, beschrieb den Mut einiger Einwohner Selmas
folgendermaßen: „Selbst dort, wo es schlecht zugeht, gibt es Menschen mit Zivilcourage."

Quartre femmes applaudissent la première manifestation pour les droits civils menée par
Martin Luther King qui partit de Selma, Alabama, pour rejoindre la capitale de cet état,
Mongomery, mars 1965. Un des leaders du mouvement, Bernard Lafayette, décrivit le
courage de certains des habitants de Selma ainsi : « Même là où la situation est terrible,
il y a des personnes courageuses ».

Four men idly watch the same march pass by. There was little they had to do to beat back the marchers – that was done for them by Sheriff Jim Clark and his deputies, and the Alabama state troopers.

Vier Männer verfolgen aufmerksam denselben vorüberziehenden Protestmarsch. Sie hatten wenig zu tun, um die Demonstranten zurückzudrängen – die Aufgabe übernahmen Sheriff Jim Clark und seine Hilfssheriffe, zusammen mit den Bundessoldaten aus Alabama.

Quatre hommes regardent négligement la même manifestation passer. Ils n'eurent pas grand-chose à faire pour repousser les manifestants – le shérif Jim Clark, ses élus et les soldats de l'état d'Alabama allaient s'en charger à leur place.

Black Panther national chairman Bobby Seale (left), with 'defence minister' Huey Newton. They were the founders of the Black Panther movement in 1966.

Der nationale Vorsitzende der Black Panther Bobby Seale (links) und sein „Verteidigungsminister" Huey Newton. Sie gründeten 1966 die Black-Panther-Bewegung.

Le président national des Black Panthers, Bobby Seale (à gauche), et son « ministre de la Défense », Huey Newton. Ils furent les membres fondateurs du mouvement des Black Panthers en 1966.

The black activist Malcolm X, 1965. In the previous year he had left the Black Muslims to set up the Organization of Afro-American Unity (OAAU). He called for a revolution, and taught that 'there can be no revolution without bloodshed'. He was murdered in February 1965.

Der Bürgerrechtsaktivist Malcolm X, 1965. Im Jahr zuvor hatte er die Gruppe der Black Muslims verlassen, um die Organisation der afro-amerikanischen Union (OAAU) zu gründen. Er rief zur Revolution auf und proklamierte, daß es „keine Revolution ohne Blutvergießen gebe". Im Februar 1965 wurde er ermordet.

L'activiste noir Malcolm X, 1965. Il quitta les Black Muslims en 1964 pour fonder l'Organisation de l'unité afro-américaine (OAAU). Il prônait la révolution et déclarait qu'il « ne pouvait y avoir de révolution sans effusion de sang ». Il fut assassiné en février 1965.

Over 200,000 people (left) gather near the Washington Memorial in August 1963 to demand equal rights for 20 million black Americans, and to hear a speech by Dr Martin Luther King. King is seen (above) in discussion with President Johnson, a year later.

Über 200.000 Menschen (links) hatten sich in der Nähe des Kapitols in Washington versammelt, um für die Gleichberechtigung der 20 Millionen schwarzen Amerikaner einzutreten und die Rede von Dr. Martin Luther King zu hören. King (oben) im Gespräch mit Präsident Johnson im darauffolgenden Jahr.

Plus de 200 000 personnes (à gauche) se réunirent près du Mémorial à Washington pour réclamer l'égalité des droits pour les 20 millions de Noirs américains et écouter le discours de Dr. Martin Luther King. Un an plus tard, King (ci-dessus) discutant avec le président Johnson.

A woman holds up a swastika during a fascist demonstration in Trafalgar Square, London, June 1962.

Eine Frau hält bei einer faschistischen Demonstration am Trafalgar Square ein Hakenkreuz hoch, London, Juni 1962.

Une femme brandissant une croix gammée lors d'une manifestation fasciste à Trafalgar Square, Londres, juin 1962.

Big on banners, small on supporters. British Nazis wave the flag at another rally in Trafalgar Square, one month later.

Große Banner, doch nur eine kleine Zahl von Anhängern. Britische Nazis hissen die Fahne auf einer anderen Kundgebung auf dem Trafalgar Square abgehalten wurde, einen Monat später.

La bannière est grande mais le nombre de partisans reste petit. Des nazis britanniques avec leur drapeau lors d'une nouvelle manifestation à Trafalgar Square, un mois plus tard.

March 1962.
London police carry
off an anti-nuclear
demonstrator
who had staged a
sit-down protest in
Parliament Square.

März 1962.
Londoner Polizisten
tragen eine Demon-
strantin weg, die vor
dem Parlament an
einem Sitzstreik
gegen Atomwaffen
teilgenommen hatte.

Mars 1962. Des
policiers londoniens
emmènent de force
une jeune femme qui
avait manifesté
contre le nucléaire
lors d'un sit-in à
Parliament Square.

March 1963. CND
supporters on one
of their many 'Ban
the Bomb' marches
from London
to Aldermaston.

März 1963. CND-
Mitglieder auf einem
ihrer zahlreichen
Märsche unter dem
Motto „Weg mit der
Bombe" von London
nach Aldermaston.

Mars 1963. Une des
nombreuses mani-
festations du mouve-
ment antinucléaire
CND revendiquant
« l'interdiction de la
bombe nucléaire »
au départ de
Londres, en route
vers Aldermaston.

An anti-Vietnam war protester kicks a policeman during
the Grosvenor Square riot outside the American Embassy
in London, 3 July 1966. Violence flared on both sides.

Während einer Demonstration gegen den Vietnamkrieg
am Grosvenor Square vor der US-Botschaft in London
versetzt ein Demonstrant einem Polizisten einen Fußtritt,
3. Juli 1966. Die Gewalt eskalierte auf beiden Seiten.

Un manifestant contre la guerre du Viêt-nam assénant un
coup de pied à un policier durant l'émeute de Grosvenor
Square devant l'ambassade américaine à Londres,
3 juillet 1966. Il y eut des violences des deux côtés.

Police cordons attempt to hold back crowds at the same riot. Although many of the demonstrators were said to be students, protest against the war came from many groups and generations.

Polizisten haben auf derselben Demonstration ein Spalier gebildet, um die aufgebrachte Menge zurückzuhalten. Die meisten der Demonstranten sollen Studenten gewesen sein, doch an der Antikriegsbewegung nahmen auch viele andere Bevölkerungs- und Altersgruppen teil.

Des cordons de police tentent de contenir la foule durant la même émeute. Bien que, selon les dires, les manifestants fussent en majorité des étudiants, il y eut parmi les contestataires des gens issus de classes et de générations très diverses.

Buenos Aires, July 1964. Argentinian police fire tear gas bombs at supporters of Juan Perón. Perón himself had fled to Spain, but the military in Argentina were always fearful that he might be returned to power in an election. In 1966 they assumed power to prevent this.

Buenos Aires, Juli 1964. Die argentinische Polizei feuert Tränengasbomben gegen Anhänger von Juan Perón ab. Perón befand sich bereits im Exil in Spanien, doch die Militärs in Argentinien befürchteten, er könne durch Wahlen wieder an die Macht gelangen. Durch einen Putsch im Jahre 1966 verhinderten sie diese Möglichkeit.

Buenos Aires, juillet 1964. La police argentine tire des grenades lacrymogènes sur les partisans de Juan Perón. Perón avait fui en Espagne mais les militaires en Argentine craignaient sans cesse qu'une élection le ramenât au pouvoir. En 1966, ils procédèrent à un coup d'Etat pour endiguer une telle évolution.

Italian demonstrators attack a member of the
Milan police, April 1969. The incident took place
during a rally called by Italian communists.

Italienische Demonstranten schlagen auf einen
Mailänder Polizisten ein, April 1969. Der Vorfall
ereignete sich auf einer Kundgebung, zu der
italienische Kommunisten aufgerufen hatten.

Des manifestants italiens attaquant un policier
milanais, avril 1969. L'incident se déroule lors
d'une manifestation organisée par les commu-
nistes italiens.

Bernadette Devlin, Independent Unity MP for Mid-Ulster, calls for support during the Battle of the Bogside in Derry (Londonderry), 14 August 1969. Devlin was then the youngest MP in Britain.

Bernadette Devlin, Parlamentsmitglied der Unabhängigkeitsunion von Mid-Ulster, ruft während der Schlacht von Bogside in Derry (Londonderry), 14. August 1969 zur Unterstützung auf. Devlin war damals das jüngste Parlamentsmitglied in Großbritannien.

Bernadette Devlin, député de l'Unité indépendante à Mid-Ulster, appelant au soutien durant la Bataille de Bogside à Derry (Londonderry), 14 août 1969. Devlin était alors le plus jeune député de Grande-Bretagne.

The man who needed no megaphone – Ian Paisley, militant
Protestant clergyman and founder of the Democratic Unionist Party,
in full cry, 22 February 1969. He had just been released from gaol.

Der Mann, der kein Megaphon brauchte – Ian Paisley, ein
militanter, protestantischer Geistlicher und Gründer der
Demokratischen Unionspartei, bei einer Ansprache, 22. Februar
1969. Er war gerade aus dem Gefängnis entlassen worden.

L'homme qui n'avait pas besoin d'un mégaphone – Ian Paisley,
protestant extrémiste, pasteur et fondateur du Parti unioniste
démocrate, lors d'un meeting, 22 février 1969. Il venait de sortir
de prison.

Derry youths prepare petrol bombs during the Battle of the Bogside, 12 August 1969. The fighting and burning in this predominantly Catholic area of the city prompted the Ulster Government to call in British troops 'to prevent a breakdown of law and order'.

Jugendliche aus Derry präparieren Benzinbomben, während der Schlacht von Bogside, 12. August 1969. Die Ausschreitungen in diesem überwiegend katholischen Stadtteil, veranlaßte die Ulster-Regierung dazu, britische Truppen zu Hilfe zu rufen, „um den Zusammenbruch von Recht und Ordnung zu verhindern".

Préparation de cocktails Molotov par des jeunes de Derry durant la Bataille de Bogside, 12 août 1969. Ce quartier, à majorité catholique, fut le théâtre de bagarres et d'incendies qui incitèrent le gouvernement d'Ulster à faire appel à l'armée britannique « pour empêcher l'effondrement de la loi et de l'ordre ».

One of the rioters hurls a blazing petrol bomb at the height of the battle, August 1969. This conflict marked the beginning of three decades of violence.

Auf dem Höhepunkt der Ausschreitungen schleudert einer der Aufständischen eine Benzinbombe, August 1969. Der Konflikt markiert den Beginn von drei Jahrzehnten der Gewalt.

Un émeutier lance un cocktail Molotov en flamme au plus fort des bagarres, août 1969. Ce conflit marqua le début de trois décennies de violence.

A member of the Royal Ulster Constabulary fights back, August 1969.
A year later the same battle was being fought in the Falls Road, Belfast. Three
years later, on Bloody Sunday, it was once again the turn of the Bogside.

Ein Polizist der Königlichen Ulster-Regierung schlägt zurück, August 1969.
Ein Jahr später ereigneten sich ähnliche Ausschreitungen in der Falls Road in
Belfast. Drei Jahre später, am Bloody Sunday, kam es erneut zu Vorfällen in
Bogside.

Un agent de la police d'Irlande du Nord rend le coup, août 1969. L'année
suivante, ce fut au tour du quartier de Falls Road à Belfast de vivre de
pareilles émeutes. Trois ans plus tard, ce fut à nouveau le tour de Bogside un
dimanche, le fameux Bloody Sunday.

12 August 1969.
In the Derry
struggle, most of the
protagonists and
most of the victims
were young.

12. August 1969.
Die meisten Prota-
gonisten und Opfer
in den Straßen-
kämpfen in Derry
waren junge Leute.

12 août 1969.
Lors de la Bataille de
Derry, la plupart des
protagonistes et des
victimes furent des
jeunes.

A dress rehearsal
for Bloody Sunday.
Violence breaks
out between civil
rights marchers
and members of the
Royal Ulster
Constabulary, Derry,
August 1969.

Eine Wiederholung
des Bloody Sundays.
Zwischen Bürger-
rechtsdemonstranten
und der Polizei der
Königlichen Ulster-
Regierung brechen
heftige Kämpfe aus,
Derry, August 1969.

Répétition générale
avant le Bloody
Sunday. Affronte-
ments entre les
manifestants pour
les droits civiques et
la police d'Irlande
du Nord, Derry,
août 1969.

4. Entertainment
Unterhaltung
Divertissements

Camille Javal, better known as Brigitte Bardot, dances in a scene
from one of her later and less successful films, *Two Weeks in September*,
October 1966. Bardot's best films were made in the Sixties.

Camille Javal, besser bekannt als Brigitte Bardot, tanzt hier in einer
Szene aus einem ihrer späteren und weniger erfolgreichen Filme, *Zwei
Wochen im September,* Oktober 1966. Bardots beste Filme entstanden
in den sechziger Jahren.

Camille Javal, plus connue sous le nom de Brigitte Bardot, dansant dans
Deux semaines en septembre, un de ses derniers et moins bons films,
octobre 1966. Les meilleurs films de Bardot datent des années soixante.

4. Entertainment
Unterhaltung
Divertissements

The cinema industry found itself in crisis in the Sixties. Television had destroyed its old confidence and had stolen its traditional audience. Television was cheap, accessible, and quick to produce – a new pop star could be on screen before the ink had dried on his contract. Film-making was comparatively slow and cumbersome, and very expensive.

So Hollywood bounced back by spending ever more money. *Ben Hur* won 11 Oscars in 1960 and set the pattern for much of the decade. Epics that followed included *El Cid*, *Lawrence of Arabia* and *Cleopatra*. More humbly, the British film industry kept going with a series of anti-hero films (*Saturday Night and Sunday Morning*, *This Sporting Life*, *Alfie*), but was shaken if not stirred when Bond came along.

Darryl F Zanuck gambled on recouping the losses he had suffered over *Cleopatra* with profits he hoped to make with *The Sound of Music*. He won. Hitchcock lost his touch but made his money with *Psycho*, *The Birds* and *Marnie*. Visconti accused 20th Century-Fox of 'destroying' *The Leopard* when they cut it from four hours to two and a half.

Towards the end of the decade, Hollywood abandoned history and entered new alien worlds with *2001: A Space Odyssey* and *Planet of the Apes*.

Die Filmindustrie steckte in den sechziger Jahren in der Krise. Das Fernsehen hatte ihr Selbstvertrauen erschüttert und ihr traditionelles Publikum abgeworben. Fernsehen war preiswert, leicht zugänglich und schnell zu produzieren – ein neuer Popstar konnte, noch bevor die Tinte auf seinem Vertrag getrocknet war, über den Bildschirm flimmern. Die Produktion von Kinofilmen war vergleichsweise zeitintensiver, schwieriger zu realisieren und kostspielig.

Doch Hollywood konterte, indem es mehr Geld als je zuvor investierte. *Ben Hur* gewann 1960 11 Oscars und wurde für dieses Jahrzehnt zum Meilenstein. Monumentalfilme wie *El Cid*,

Lawrence von Arabien und *Cleopatra* folgten. Weitaus bescheidener hingegen fuhr die britische Filmindustrie mit einer Serie von Filmen mit Antihelden *(Saturday Night and Sunday Morning, This Sporting Life, Alfie)* fort, doch mit James Bond kam wieder Wind ins englische Kino.

Darryl F. Zanuck hatte mit der Produktion von *Cleopatra* schwere Verluste einstecken müssen, mit *The Sound of Music* hoffte er, diese wieder einfahren zu können. Er hatte richtig kalkuliert. Obwohl Hitchcock von seinem magischen Zauber verloren hatte, bescherten ihm *Psycho*, *Die Vögel* und *Marnie* volle Kinokassen. Visconti beschuldigte die 20th Century Fox, seinen Film *Der Leopard* „zerstört" zu haben, indem sie ihn von vier auf zweieinhalb Stunden gekürzt hatten.

Gegen Ende des Jahrzehnts hatte Hollywood sich vom Historiengenre verabschiedet und mit *2001: Odyssee im Weltraum* und *Planet der Affen* neue, fremde Welten für sich entdeckt.

Pour l'industrie du cinéma, les années soixante furent une période de crise. La télévision avait ébranlé sa confiance et détourné son public traditionnel. Elle était bon marché, à la portée de tous et vite produite – une nouvelle star de la musique pop pouvait naître sur le petit écran avant même que l'encre de son contrat ne soit sèche. La réalisation d'un film était au contraire lente, difficile et très coûteuse.

Hollywood décida de réagir en dépensant plus d'argent que jamais. *Ben Hur* remporta 11 Oscars en 1960 et, ce faisant, définit le style de presque tous les films de la décennie. Il y eut ainsi d'autres films à grand spectacle comme *Le Cid*, *Lawrence d'Arabie* et *Cléopâtre*. Plus modeste, l'industrie du film britannique continuait à produire des films d'antihéros *(Saturday Night and Sunday Morning, This Sporting Life, Alfie)* mais elle fut ébranlée, pour en pas dire transformée, avec l'arrivée des films de James Bond.

Darryl F. Zanuck misa sur les bénéfices qu'il espérait tirer de *La Mélodie du bonheur* pour surmonter les pertes subies avec *Cléopâtre* et gagna son pari. Hitchcock, qui avait perdu un peu de sa touche magique, connut le succès commercial grâce à *Psycho*, *Les oiseaux* et *Marnie*. Visconti accusa la 20th Century-Fox d'avoir « démoli » *Le Guépard* en procédant à des coupures qui ramenèrent le film de quatre heures à deux heures et demie.

Vers la fin de la décennie, Hollywood abandonna l'histoire pour se tourner vers des nouveaux mondes étranges et produisit *2001 : L'Odyssée de l'espace* et *La Planète des singes*.

Jeanne Moreau
at a press conference
where she announced
her marriage to the
fashion designer
Pierre Cardin, 1962.

Jeanne Moreau auf
einer Pressekonfe-
renz, bei der sie ihre
Heirat mit dem
Modedesigner Pierre
Cardin bekannt gab,
1962.

Jeanne Moreau lors
d'une conférence de
presse au cours de
laquelle elle annonça
son mariage avec le
couturier Pierre
Cardin, 1962.

Romy Schneider on
set at the disused
Gare St Lazare,
Paris, during the
filming of Orson
Welles' *The Trial*,
based on Kafka's
novel, 1962.

Romy Schneider am
Set des stillgelegten
Bahnhofs St. Lazare,
Paris, während der
Dreharbeiten zu
Orson Welles' *Der
Prozeß*, basierend auf
Kafkas Roman,
1962.

Romy Schneider
dans le décor de la
Gare St-Lazare
désaffectée, Paris,
pendant le tournage
du film d'Orson
Welles *Le Procès*, tiré
du roman de Kafka,
1962.

Peter Sellers and
Sophia Loren in
what the critics
regarded as a
travesty of Shaw's
comedy, *The
Millionairess*, 1960.

Peter Sellers und
Sophia Loren in *Die
Millionärin*, den die
Kritiker für eine
Verzerrung von
Shaws gleichnamiger
Komödie hielten,
1960.

Peter Sellers et
Sophia Loren dans
La Millionnaire qui,
selon la critique,
était une satire de la
comédie de Shaw,
1960.

Marilyn Monroe in *Let's Make Love*, 1960.
'I seem to be a whole superstructure with
no foundation,' said Monroe. 'I'm working
on the foundation.'

Marilyn Monroe in *Let's Make Love*, 1960.
Die Monroe sagte von sich: „Ich komme
mir vor wie ein Oberbau ohne Fundament.
Auf dieser Grundlage arbeite ich."

Marilyn Monroe dans *Le Milliardaire*,
1960. « Je me sens comme une maison sans
fondations », déclara Monroe. « J'ai décidé
de m'attaquer aux fondations ».

Jean-Paul Belmondo arrives at Nice Airport with Ursula Andress, December 1968.
He was there to work on *La Sirène du Mississippi* with Catherine Deneuve. The film
was later described as 'interesting and uncomfortable'.

Jean-Paul Belmondo kommt zusammen mit Ursula Andress auf dem Flughafen in
Nizza an, Dezember 1968. Er arbeitete dort mit Catherine Deneuve an *Das Geheimnis
der falschen Braut*. Den Film beurteilte man später als „interessant und anstrengend".

Arrivée de Jean-Paul Belmondo à l'aéroport de Nice en compagnie d'Ursula Andress,
décembre 1968. Il était là pour tourner *La Sirène du Mississippi* avec Catherine
Deneuve, un film qui fut par la suite jugé « intéressant et dérangeant ».

Jane Fonda helps Alain Delon to blow out the 28 candles on his birthday cake, 11 November 1963. They were filming *Ni saints, ni saufs*.

Jane Fonda hilft Alain Delon, die 28 Kerzen auf seiner Geburtstagstorte auszublasen, 11. November 1963. Sie drehten gemeinsam *Ni saints, ni saufs*.

Jane Fonda aide Alain Delon à souffler les 28 bougies de son gâteau d'anniversaire, 11 novembre 1963. Ils tournaient ensemble *Ni saints, ni saufs*.

(Above) Richard Burton takes Elizabeth Taylor's hand at a screening of *Lawrence of Arabia*, 26 March 1963. (Right) Burton and Taylor on the set of *Cleopatra*. 'Acting is a kind of showing off,' said Burton. 'And the best person to show off to is your wife.'

(Oben) Richard Burton hält die Hand von Elizabeth Taylor während der Vorführung von *Laurence von Arabien*, 26. März 1963. (Rechts) Das Paar Burton und Taylor bei den Dreharbeiten zu *Cleopatra*. „Vor der Kamera stehen, ist eine Möglichkeit, sich vorteilhaft zur Geltung zu bringen", sagte Burton, „und am besten bringt man sich gegenüber der eigenen Frau zur Geltung."

(Ci-dessus) Richard Burton prend la main d'Elizabeth Taylor lors d'une projection de *Lawrence d'Arabie*, 26 mars 1963. (A droite) Burton et Taylor sur le plateau de *Cléopâtre*. « Jouer, c'est un peu comme essayer de séduire », disait Burton « et, la personne idéale à séduire, c'est sa femme ».

Elizabeth Taylor leaves London for California, 27 March 1961. Less than two weeks earlier she had almost died in a London hotel. 'You feel yourself falling into a horrible black pit. You hear a screaming jet noise. Your skin is falling off… I fought so hard to live.'

Elizabeth Taylor verläßt London, um nach Kalifornien zurückzukehren, 27. März 1961. Knapp zwei Wochen vor ihrer Abreise wäre sie beinahe in einem Londoner Hotel gestorben. „Man fühlt sich, als würde man in ein unheimliches, schwarzes Loch fallen. Man hört einen ohrenbetäubenden Lärm und die Haut löst sich auf … Ich habe sehr um mein Leben gekämpft."

Elizabeth Taylor quitte Londres pour la Californie, 27 mars 1961. Deux semaines plus tôt, elle avait failli mourir dans un hôtel londonien. « Vous vous sentez tomber dans un horrible trou noir. Vous entendez un long cri perçant. Votre peau se décolle … J'ai dû me battre de toutes mes forces pour vivre ».

Vera Jane Palmer, better known as Jayne Mansfield, 1965. Although many regarded her as a second-rate Marilyn Monroe, Mansfield was an intelligent actress who suffered from being habitually cast as a dumb blonde.

Vera Jane Palmer, besser bekannt als Jayne Mansfield, 1965. Viele hielten sie für eine zweitklassige Marilyn Monroe, doch Jayne Mansfield war eine intelligente Schauspielerin, die darunter litt, immer wieder das dumme Blondchen mimen zu müssen.

Vera Jane Palmer, mieux connue sous le nom de Jayne Mansfield, 1965. Bien que beaucoup de gens virent en elle une Marilyn Monroe de deuxième classe, Mansfield était une actrice intelligente qui souffrit d'être cantonnée dans des rôles de blonde idiote.

Catherine Deneuve
and her husband, the
photographer David
Bailey, arrive at the
Royal Première of
Born Free, 12 March
1966.

Catherine Deneuve
und ihr Ehemann,
der Fotograf David
Bailey, treffen zur
königlichen Premiere
des Films *Born Free*
ein, 12. März 1966.

Catherine Deneuve
et son mari, le
photographe David
Bailey, à leur arrivée
à la première royale
de *Né libre*, 12 mars
1966.

Polish film director
Roman Polanski
and American actress
Sharon Tate after
their wedding,
20 January 1968.
Fifteen months later
she was murdered.

Der polnische Re-
gisseur Roman
Polanski und die
amerikanische
Schauspielerin
Sharon Tate kurz
nach ihrer Hochzeit,
20. Januar 1968.
Fünfzehn Monate
später wurde sie
ermordet.

Le metteur en scène
polonais Roman
Polanski et l'actrice
américaine Sharon
Tate juste après leur
mariage, 20 janvier
1968. Tate fut
assassinée 15 mois
plus tard.

Steve McQueen and his wife Neile, during a break in the filming
of *Bullitt*, August 1968. 'In my own mind,' said McQueen, 'I'm not
sure that acting is something a grown man should be doing.'

Steve McQueen und seine Ehefrau Neile während einer Pause zu
den Dreharbeiten von *Bullitt*, August 1968. „Ich glaube eigentlich
nicht," meinte McQueen, „daß der Beruf des Schauspielers für
einen erwachsenen Mann das Richtige ist."

Steve McQueen et sa femme Neile durant une pause sur le tournage de *Bullitt*, août 1968. « En ce qui me concerne », déclara
McQueen, « je ne suis pas sûr que le métier d'acteur soit fait pour
les adultes ».

Beau Bridges and Lee Grant, on location in Brooklyn during the making of *The Landlord*, September 1969. The film was not a success. 'Not an avenue of offensiveness to any race is left unexplored,' said one critic.

Beau Bridges und Lee Grant während der Dreharbeiten in Brooklyn zu *Der Hausbesitzer*, September 1969. Der Film war ein Flop. „Keine Möglichkeit wurde ausgelassen, andere Rassen zu verunglimpfen …", erklärte ein Kritiker.

Beau Bridges et Lee Grant à Brooklyn sur le tournage d'une scène de *The Landlord*, septembre 1969. Le film n'eut aucun succès. « Personne ni aucune race n'est épargnée, le film se moque de tout le monde », expliqua un critique.

Woody Allen and Ursula Andress, stars of *What's New Pussycat?*, at the film's Royal Gala Performance, Leicester Square, London, March 1966.

Woody Allen und Ursula Andress, die Stars von *What's New Pussycat?*, bei der Premierenvorstellung, Leicester Square, London, März 1966.

Woody Allen et Ursula Andress, les vedettes de *What's New Pussycat?*, à la première du film, Leicester Square, Londres, mars 1966.

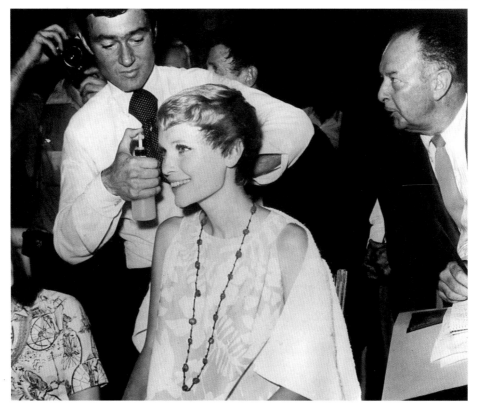

Vidal Sassoon gives Mia Farrow a £500 haircut, 1968. Farrow was about to make *Rosemary's Baby*, the first Hollywood film directed by Roman Polanski. The film, about a woman who believes the Devil has fathered her child, repelled, thrilled and fascinated audiences.

Mia Farrows Haarschnitt von Vidal Sassoon hat 500 Pfund gekostet, 1968. Farrow sollte bald mit den Dreharbeiten zu *Rosemaries Baby* beginnen, dem ersten Hollywood-Film von Roman Polanski. Der Film handelt von einer schwangeren Frau, die glaubt, der Teufel sei der Vater ihres Kindes und rief bei den Zuschauern Abscheu, Schrecken und Begeisterung hervor.

Une coupe Vidal Sassoon à 500 £ pour Mia Farrow, 1968. Elle allait bientôt tourner *Rosemary's Baby*, le premier film de Roman Polanski à Hollywood. Ce film, dans lequel une femme croit que le père de son enfant est le diable suscita à la fois répulsion, fascination et enthousiasme auprès du public.

Judy Garland leaves Heathrow Airport, London, with her fiancé, Micky Deans, 1968.
Deans was the manager of Arthur's, a fashionable disco in Manhattan. Garland had come
to London to play the Palladium, but she was too sick to work. A year later, she was dead.

Judy Garland verläßt den Flughafen Heathrow, London, mit ihrem Verlobten Mickey
Deans, 1968. Deans war der Geschäftsführer der In-Diskothek Arthur's in Manhattan.
Die Garland war nach London gekommen, um im Palladium zu spielen. Doch sie war zu
krank, um zu arbeiten. Ein Jahr später starb sie.

Judy Garland quitte l'aéroport de Heathrow, Londres, avec son fiancé, Micky Deans,
1968. Deans était le gérant d'Arthur's, une boîte de nuit à la mode de Manhattan.
Garland était venue à Londres pour chanter au Palladium mais fut trop malade pour
travailler. Elle mourut l'année suivante.

Yugoslav actress Sonia Romanoff attacks paparazzo photographer Rino Barillari with an ice cream, Rome, 1966. He had taken an unflattering picture of her.

Die jugoslawische Schauspielerin Sonia Romanoff attackiert den Paparazzo Rino Barillari mit ihrem Eis, Rom, 1966. Er hatte ein nicht besonders schmeichelhaftes Foto von ihr gemacht.

L'actrice yougoslave Sonia Romanoff agresse Rino Barillari, un paparazzo, avec une glace, Rome, 1966. Il venait de prendre une photo d'elle peu flatteuse.

The French director Jean-Luc Godard during the filming of *One Plus One*, 1968.
The film featured the Rolling Stones, in a plot made up of the parallel themes of
'construction and destruction'. During filming, the studio burnt down.

Der französische Regisseur Jean-Luc Godard während der Dreharbeiten zu *Eins
plus Eins*, 1968. Der Film zeigt die Rolling Stones in einer Geschichte, die um die
Themen von „Konstruktion und Destruktion" kreist. Während der Dreharbeiten
brannte das Studio ab.

Le cinéaste français Jean-Luc Godard sur le tournage de *Week-end*, 1968. Le film
mettait en scène les Rolling Stones dans une intrigue basée sur les thèmes parallèles
de la « construction et de la destruction ». Le studio brûla pendant le tournage.

Orson Welles, Paris, 1962. 'All of us will always owe him everything' – Jean-Luc Godard on Welles.

Orson Welles, Paris, 1962. „Jeder von uns wird ihm immer alles zu verdanken haben", sagte Jean-Luc Godard über Orson Welles.

Orson Welles, Paris, 1962. « Nous lui devrons toujours tout » déclara Jean-Luc Godard à propos de Welles.

A picture by Erich Auerbach of Count Luchino Visconti, 1966. Visconti's two great films of the Sixties were *The Leopard* and *The Damned*. Critics accused him of making films that increasingly looked like operas without music.

Graf Luchino Visconti fotografiert von Erich Auerbach, 1966. Visconti drehte zwei große Filme in den sechziger Jahren, *Der Leopard* und *Die Verdammten*. Die Kritiker warfen ihm vor, er mache Filme, die in Wirklichkeit Opern seien, nur ohne Musik.

Le comte Luchino Visconti photographié par Erich Auerbach, 1966. Visconti réalisa deux films magnifiques au cours des années soixante, *Le Guépard* et *Les Damnés*. Les critiques l'accusèrent de faire des films qui ressemblaient de plus en plus à des opéras sans musique.

Federico Fellini at the launch of his film *La Dolce Vita* in Paris, 16 April 1960. The film received critical approval and papal condemnation.

Federico Fellini in Paris, kurz vor dem Kinostart seines Films *Das süße Leben*, Paris, 16. April 1960. Der Film wurde von der Kritik begeistert aufgenommen und vom Papst verdammt.

Federico Fellini lors du lancement de son film *La Dolce Vita*, Paris, 16 avril 1960. Le film fut applaudi par la critique et condamné par le pape.

Founder members of
the Rat Pack, Dean
Martin (centre) and
Frank Sinatra arrive
at London Airport,
4 July 1961.

Gründungsmit-
glieder der Rat Pack,
Dean Martin (Mitte)
und Frank Sinatra,
kommen am
Londoner Flughafen
an, 4. Juli 1961.

L'arrivée des mem-
bres fondateurs du
Rat Pack, Dean
Martin (au centre) et
Frank Sinatra, aéro-
port de Londres,
4 juillet 1961.

Another member of the Pack, Sammy Davis Junior (left), with the American comedian Jack Benny, 6 November 1961. They were rehearsing their contributions to the Royal Variety Show at the Prince of Wales Theatre, London.

Ein weiteres Mitglied der Pack, Sammy Davis Jr. (links), mit dem amerikanischen Komödianten Jack Benny, 6. November 1961. Sie proben ihren Beitrag zu der Royal Variety Show im Prince of Wales Theatre, London.

Un autre membre du Pack, Sammy Davis junior (à gauche) avec le comique américain Jack Benny, 6 novembre 1961. Ils répétaient leurs numéros pour le Royal Variety Show au Prince of Wales Theatre de Londres.

December 1964.
British actress Diana
Rigg as Emma Peel
in the cult television
series *The Avengers*.

Dezember 1964.
Die englische Schau-
spielerin Diana Rigg
wurde als Emma
Peel in der Fernseh-
serie *Mit Schirm,
Charme und Melone*
berühmt.

Décembre 1964.
L'actrice britannique
Diana Rigg dans le
rôle d'Emma Peel
dans *Chapeau melon
et bottes de cuir*, la
série de télévision
culte.

James Fox (left) and Mick Jagger on the set of the film *Performance*, 1969.
'You don't have to be a drug addict, pederast, sado-masochist or nitwit to enjoy
it,' wrote John Simon, 'but being one or more of these things would help.'

James Fox (links) und Mick Jagger während der Dreharbeiten zu dem Film
Performance, 1969. „Um hier Spaß zu haben, muß man keine Drogen nehmen,
man muß auch kein Päderast, Masochist oder Schwachkopf sein", schrieb John
Simon, „obwohl eine oder mehrere dieser Personen zu sein, helfen würde."

James Fox (à gauche) et Mick Jagger sur le plateau du film *Performance*, 1969.
« Il n'est pas nécessaire d'être un drogué, un pédéraste, un sadomasochiste ou
un imbécile pour l'apprécier », écrivit John Simon, « mais d'être une ou
plusieurs de ces personnes peut aider ».

'An honest man's word is as good as his bond.' George Lazenby's wasn't very good – here he is relaxing on the set of *On Her Majesty's Secret Service*, November 1968.

„Das Wort eines ehrlichen Mannes gilt soviel wie eine Bürgschaft." Für George Lazenby traf dies nicht unbedingt zu – er entspannt sich hier bei den Dreharbeiten zu *Im Geheimauftrag Ihrer Majestät*, November 1968.

« Rien ne vaut la parole d'un honnête homme » dit la maxime. George Lazenby, qui fut un piètre James Bond, fait une pause pendant le tournage du film *Au service de sa Majesté*, novembre 1968.

Sean Connery's Bond was the best. This is a scene from *You Only Live Twice*, Pinewood Studios, 1966.

Der beste James Bond war Sean Connery. Dies ist eine Szene aus *Du lebst nur zweimal*, Pinewood Studios, 1966.

Sean Connery fut le meilleur des James Bond. Voici une scène tirée du film *On ne vit que deux fois*, les studios de Pinewood, 1966.

Newlyweds Cilla Black and Bobby Willis, 1969. Black had many recording hits in the Sixties, of which perhaps the best-known was *Alfie*. Willis was her manager. Despite appearances here, the marriage has been an extremely happy one over 30 years.

Die Jungvermählten Cilla Black und Bobby Willis, 1969. Sie war in den sechziger Jahren ein bekannter Schlagerstar und landete ihren größten Hit mit *Alfie*. Willis war ihr Manager. Auch wenn es hier nicht so aussieht, führten die beiden über 30 Jahre lang eine glückliche Ehe.

Cilla Black et Bobby Willis jeunes mariés, 1969. Black enregistra un grand nombre de chansons qui furent des tubes dans les années soixante, mais la plus connue reste peut-être *Alfie*. Willis fut son manager. En dépit des apparences, leur mariage fut très heureux et dura plus de 30 ans.

The English comedian Benny Hill, January 1960. Hill's television programmes became unaccountably popular in many parts of the world.

Der englische Komiker Benny Hill, Januar 1960. Hills Fernsehbeiträge machten ihn in weiten Teilen der Welt bekannt und unglaublich beliebt.

Le comique anglais Benny Hill, janvier 1960. Les émissions télévisées de Benny Hill connurent un succès énorme aux quatre coins du monde.

October 1963. British film star Julie Christie (seated) in her Birmingham bedsit. With her is landlady Mrs Dorothy Cetti.

Oktober 1963. Die englische Schauspielerin Julie Christie (sitzend) bewohnt ein möbliertes Zimmer in Birmingham. Ihre Zimmerwirtin war Mrs. Dorothy Cetti.

Octobre 1963. La vedette du cinéma britannique Julie Christie (assise) dans sa chambre meublée de Birmingham en compagnie de sa logeuse, Mme Dorothy Cetti.

Michael Caine (centre) with his mother and brother, at home in Bermondsey, London, 1964. Caine was the first of the English working-class romantic screen heroes. 'He has the gift,' wrote Pauline Kael, 'of conveying what his character is thinking without excess motion.'

Michael Caine (Mitte) mit seiner Mutter und seinem Bruder zu Hause in Bermondsey, London, 1964. Caine war der erste romantische Filmheld, der aus der englischen Arbeiterklasse stammte. „Er besitzt das Talent," schrieb Pauline Kael, „das Wesen der Charaktere, die er spielt zu offenbaren, ohne übertriebene Gesten machen zu müssen."

Michael Caine (au centre) avec sa mère et son frère chez eux à Bermondsey, Londres, 1964. Caine fut le premier héros romantique du cinéma à être issu de la classe ouvrière anglaise. « Il a le don », écrivait Pauline Kael, « de montrer ce que pense son personnage sans en faire trop ».

5. The Arts
Die Kunst
Les arts

Rudolf Nureyev, 1967. Nureyev was granted political asylum in Paris in 1961, where he joined the Grand Ballet du Marquis de Cuevas. He made his Covent Garden debut in 1962 with British ballerina Margot Fonteyn, whose career he rekindled.

Rudolf Nurejew, 1967. Nachdem ihm 1961 in Paris politisches Asyl gewährt worden war, schloß er sich dem Pariser Grand Ballet du Marquis de Cuevas an. 1962 hatte er seinen ersten Auftritt in Covent Garden zusammen mit der britischen Ballerina Margot Fonteyn, die ein Comeback feiern konnte.

Rudolf Noureïev, 1967. Noureïev obtint l'asile politique à Paris en 1961, où il entra au Grand Ballet du Marquis de Cuevas. Pour ses débuts à Covent Garden en 1962, il dansa avec la danseuse britannique Margot Fonteyn dont la carrière connut ainsi un second souffle.

5. The Arts
   Die Kunst
   Les arts

In the Sixties, new life was injected into the arts, and new styles developed. There was an air of joyous experimentation that produced the good, the bad and the ugly. Pop artists and Beat poets revelled in the triumph of presentation over content, but it was all rich food for thought. The rock musical *Hair* presented nudity on stage, some attractive songs, and transcendental images that proved to be profitable at the box office.

The art world began to wake up to the fortunes that could be made from paintings. In Paris, an exhibition of Picasso's work in 1967 drew hundreds of thousands of visitors. The National Gallery of Art in Washington DC paid $5 million for *Ginevra dei Benci* by Leonardo da Vinci – then the highest price ever paid for a single painting.

Joseph Heller published *Catch-22* in 1961, and delighted thousands of readers. Rachel Carson published *Silent Spring* in 1962, disturbed many of her readers, and infuriated the agrochemical industry. She died of cancer two years later.

Grandma Moses, the self-trained painter, died at the age of 101. Edith Piaf, the Parisian songstress, died at the age of 47. Andy Warhol was shot by Valerie Solanis, founder of SCUM (the Society for Cutting Up Men), but survived. Ernest Hemingway shot himself, and didn't.

In den sechziger Jahren kam in die Kunstszene neues Leben, und es entwickelten sich neue Stilrichtungen. In der Luft lag eine Experimentierfreude, die Gutes, Schlechtes und Häßliches hervorbrachte. Die Pop-art-Künstler und die Dichter der Beat-Generation feierten den Triumpf der Form über den Inhalt, und regten damit maßgeblich zum Nachdenken an. Das Rockmusical *Hair* zeigte nackte Körper auf der Bühne, brachte einige gute Songs, die ins Blut gingen, und Bilder einer weltentrückten Stimmung, die dafür sorgten, daß die Kinokassen sich füllten.

In der Welt der bildenden Kunst begann man zu erkennen, daß mit der Malerei ein

Vermögen zu verdienen war. Mehrere hunderttausend Besucher strömten 1967 in eine Picasso-Ausstellung in Paris. Die National Gallery of Art in Washington D.C. zahlte für Leonardo da Vincis *Ginevra dei Benci* fünf Millionen US-Dollar – das war in der damaligen Zeit die höchste Summe, die je für ein Bild bezahlt worden war.

Joseph Heller begeisterte 1961 mit seinem Buch *Catch-22* Tausende von Lesern. Rachel Carson veröffentlichte 1962 *Silent Spring*, mit dem sie viele ihrer Leser beunruhigte und die Verärgerung der agrochemischen Industrie auf sich zog. Zwei Jahre später starb sie an Krebs.

Die Malerin Grandma Moses, eine Autodidaktin, starb im Alter von 101 Jahren. Die französische Chansonsängerin Edith Piaf starb bereits im Alter von nur 47 Jahren. Andy Warhol überlebte die Schüsse, die Valerie Solanis, Gründerin der SCUM (Gesellschaft zur Vernichtung der Männer), auf ihn abgefeuert hatte. Anders, Ernest Hemingway, der sich mit einer Kugel das Leben nahm.

Dans les années soixante, les arts connurent un élan neuf et de nouveaux styles se développèrent. Ce fut une époque d'expérimentations joyeuses qui donna lieu à des résultats aussi bons que mauvais ou franchement terribles. Les artistes pop et les poètes de la Beat génération prenaient grand plaisir à faire triompher la forme sur le contenu, l'essentiel étant de faire réfléchir. La comédie musicale *Hair* exposa la nudité sur scène avec quelques bonnes chansons et des images transcendantales qui se révélèrent un grand succès au box-office.

Le monde des arts prit soudain conscience que la peinture pouvait rapporter des fortunes. A Paris, en 1967, une exposition de Picasso attira des centaines de milliers de visiteurs. A Washington D.C., la National Gallery of Art s'offrit le *Ginevra dei Benci* de Léonard de Vinci pour 5 millions de dollars – ce fut, à l'époque, le prix le plus élevé jamais payé pour un tableau.

En 1961, Joseph Heller publia *Catch-22* et enchanta des milliers de lecteurs. En 1962, le livre de Rachel Carson, *Silent Spring*, troubla un grand nombre de ses lecteurs et lui attira les foudres de l'industrie agrochimique. Elle mourut d'un cancer deux ans plus tard.

Grandma Moses, la célèbre peintre autodidacte, mourut à l'âge de 101 ans et Edith Piaf, la célèbre chanteuse parisienne, à l'âge de 47 ans. Andy Warhol survécut aux coups de feu tirés par Valerie Solanis, la fondatrice de SCUM (Association pour le dépeçage des hommes). Ernest Hemingway se tira une balle et n'y survécut pas.

January 1968. American Pop artist Roy Lichtenstein stands in front of his painting *Whaam!*, on show at the Tate Gallery, London. Lichtenstein was a major figure in the Pop art movement, specializing in enlarged versions of pictures from magazines and comic strips.

Januar 1968. Der amerikanische Popkünstler Roy Lichtenstein steht vor seinem Gemälde *Whaam!* in der Tate Gallery, London. Lichtenstein gehörte zu den bedeutendsten Figuren der Pop-art. Die Bildthemen für seine überdimensional großen und weltbekannten Werke entnahm er Zeitschriften und Comic strips.

Janvier 1968. L'artiste pop américain, Roy Lichtenstein, devant son tableau *Whaam!* exposé à la Tate Gallery, Londres. Lichtenstein fut une figure de proue du mouvement de l'art pop. Il travaillait essentiellement à partir d'agrandissements de photos extraites de journaux et de bandes dessinées.

David Hockney in 1965. Hockney spent much of the Sixties in the United States. He based his series of etchings, *The Rake's Progress*, on his adventures in New York, and taught at the University of California from 1965 to 1967.

David Hockney im Jahre 1965. Hackney verbrachte den Großteil der sechziger Jahre in den USA. Seine Erlebnisse in New York bildeten die Grundlage für die Serie von Radierungen *The Rake's Progress*. Von 1965 bis 1967 lehrte er an der Universität von Kalifornien.

David Hockney en 1965. Hockney passa la plus grande partie des années soixante aux Etats-Unis. Sa série de gravures, *The Rake's Progress*, fut inspirée par ses aventures à New York. Il enseigna à l'université de Californie de 1965 à 1967.

Pop artist and film-maker Andy Warhol. The Sixties produced some of his most famous work, including the *Campbell's Soup Can* series, and the film *Chelsea Girls*.

Der Pop-art-Künstler und Filmemacher Andy Warhol. In den sechziger Jahren schuf er einige seiner größten Werke wie die Serie *Campbell's Soup Can* und den Film *Chelsea Girls*.

L'artiste pop et réalisateur Andy Warhol. Il créa durant les années soixante quelques-unes de ses œuvres les plus célèbres, dont la série de peintures *Campbell's Soup Can* et le film *Chelsea Girls*.

American author Ken Elton Kesey, May 1969. Kesey was a writer associated with the Beat generation, and author of *One Flew Over the Cuckoo's Nest* (1963), based on his experiences as a ward attendant in a mental hospital.

Der amerikanische Autor Ken Elton Kesey, Mai 1969. Kesey, der der Beat Generation angehörte, schrieb *Einer flog über das Kuckucksnest* (1963). Die Geschichte basiert auf seinen Erfahrungen als Krankenpfleger auf einer Station in einer Nervenheilanstalt.

L'auteur américain Ken Elton Kesey, mai 1969. Kesey, qui fit partie de la Beat génération, écrivit *Vol au-dessus d'un nid de coucous* (1963) en s'inspirant de son expérience de garçon de salle dans un hôpital psychiatrique.

The high priests
of hippiedom.
Dr Timothy Leary
(centre) in
conference with
Abbie Hoffman (left)
and Jerry Rubin
(right), New York
City, February 1968.

Die Hohepriester
des Hippietums.
Dr. Timothy Leary
(Mitte) auf einer
Konferenz mit Abbie
Hoffman (links) und
Jerry Rubin (rechts),
New York, Februar
1968.

Les grands prêtres
du mouvement
hippie. Le docteur
Timothy Leary
(au centre) lors
d'une conférence,
avec Abbie Hoffman
(à gauche) et Jerry
Rubin (à droite),
New York, février
1968.

Norman Mailer (left), American journalist, novelist and polemicist, with writer
Henry Miller, 1962. Mailer wrote a series of books against the Vietnam War
during the Sixties, including *Why Are We in Vietnam?* and *Armies of the Night*.

Norman Mailer (links), amerikanischer Journalist, Schriftsteller und Polemiker,
zusammen mit dem Schriftsteller Henry Miller, 1962. In den sechziger Jahren
bezog Mailer in einer Reihe von Büchern kritisch Stellung gegen den Vietnamkrieg, darunter *Am Beispiel einer Bärenjagd?* und in *Heere aus der Nacht*.

Norman Mailer (à gauche), journaliste, écrivain et polémiste américain en
compagnie de l'écrivain Henry Miller, 1962. Mailer écrivit au cours des années
soixante une série de livres contre la guerre du Viêt-nam, dont *Pourquoi
sommes-nous au Viêt-nam ?* et *Les Armées de la nuit*.

Allen Ginsberg (right) and Gary Snyder, American poets of the Beat generation, 1962. Snyder advocated simple living and hard physical work. Ginsberg advocated experimentation with drugs.

Allen Ginsberg (rechts) und Gary Snyder, amerikanische Schriftsteller der Beat Generation, 1962. Snyder empfahl ein einfaches Leben und harte körperliche Arbeit. Ginsberg trat für Drogenexperimente ein.

Allen Ginsberg (à droite) et Gary Snyder, des poètes américains de la génération Beat, 1962. Snyder préconisait un mode de vie simple impliquant un travail physique dur. Ginsberg défendait les expériences de drogues diverses.

American playwright Arthur Miller, December 1965. In 1961 Miller wrote *The Misfits*, his ex-wife Marilyn Monroe's last film. 'I was prepared to dedicate a year of my life to her enhancement as a performer... I would never have dreamed of writing a movie otherwise.'

Der amerikanische Dramatiker Arthur Miller, Dezember 1965. Miller schrieb 1961 *Nicht gesell-schaftsfähig*, in dem Marilyn Monroe, seine Ex-Frau, ihre letzte Rolle spielte. „Ich hatte mich darauf eingestellt, ein Jahr meines Lebens ihrem Engagement als Schauspielerin zu widmen ... Ich wäre sonst nie auf die Idee gekommen, ein Filmdrehbuch zu schreiben."

Le dramaturge américain Arthur Miller, décembre 1965. En 1961, Miller écrivit *Les Désaxés*, qui fut le dernier film dans lequel joua son ex-femme, Marilyn Monroe. « J'étais prêt à consacrer un an de ma vie pour la mettre en valeur en tant qu'actrice ... je n'aurais jamais songé à écrire un film autrement ».

The Irish playwright
Samuel Beckett,
Paris, June 1961.
Beckett won the
Nobel Prize for
Literature in 1969.

Der irische Schrift-
steller Samuel
Beckett, Paris, Juni
1961. Beckett erhielt
1969 den Nobelpreis
für Literatur.

Le dramaturge
irlandais Samuel
Beckett, Paris, juin
1961. Beckett reçut
le prix Nobel de
littérature en 1969.

Beetlemania. Steven Berkoff, British playwright, actor and director, performing in his own adaptation of Kafka's *Metamorphosis* at the Roundhouse Theatre, London, 1969. His role was that of a young man who is transformed into a beetle.

Beetlemania. Steven Berkoff, britischer Dramatiker, Schauspieler und Theaterintendant in einer Inszenierung von Kafkas *Die Verwandlung* im Roundhouse Theatre, London, 1969. Er selbst spielte den jungen Mann, der sich in einen Käfer verwandelte.

Insecte-folie. Steven Berkoff, dramaturge, acteur et metteur en scène britannique, jouant sa propre adaptation de *La Métamorphose* de Kafka au Roundhouse Theatre, Londres, 1969. Il incarnait un jeune homme qui se transforme en insecte.

Trevor Nunn, successor to Peter Hall as artistic director of the Royal Shakespeare Company, 1968.

Trevor Nunn, Nachfolger des künstlerischen Leiters Peter Hall in der Royal Shakespeare Company, 1968.

Trevor Nunn, le successeur de Peter Hall à la direction artistique de la Royal Shakespeare Company, 1968.

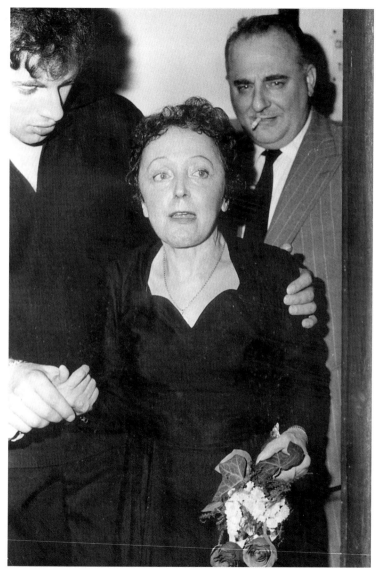

The Little Sparrow –
Edith Piaf, perhaps
the most popular
French singer of all
time, 1960.

Der kleine Spatz –
Edith Piaf, die wohl
beliebteste französi-
sche Sängerin aller
Zeiten, 1960.

La môme – Edith
Piaf, peut-être la
plus grande figure de
la chanson française
de tous les temps,
1960.

The Austrian singer
Lotte Lenya, March
1961. Her husky
voice was once
described as being
'one octave below
laryngitis'.

Die österreichische
Sängerin Lotte
Lenya, März 1961.
Ihre rauhe Stimme
wurde einmal als
„eine Oktave tiefer
als bei einer Kehl-
kopfentzündung"
beschrieben.

La chanteuse
autrichienne Lotte
Lenya, mars 1961.
On disait de sa voix
rauque qu'elle « était
un octave en-dessous
de la laryngite ».

Erich Auerbach's portrait of the jazz pianist, composer and bandleader
Thelonious Sphere Monk, April 1961. Monk was a larger-than-life
figure, whose humour was revealed in his highly original and percussive
style of piano playing.

Erich Auerbach porträtierten den Jazzpianisten, Komponisten und Bandleader Thelonious Sphere Monk, April 1961. Monk war eine überlebens-
große Erscheinung, dessen Humor sich in der ungewöhnlichen und
kraftvollen Art, wie er die Tasten des Klaviers anschlug, offenbarte.

Le pianiste de jazz, compositeur et chef d'orchestre Thelonious Sphere
Monk photographié par Erich Auerbach, avril 1961. Monk était
une figure plus grande que nature dont l'humour transparassait dans
sa manière de jouer au piano à la fois très originale et percutante.

American jazz pianist
Dave Brubeck (left)
encouraging a young
bass player, 1962.

Der amerikanische
Jazzpianist Dave
Brubeck (links)
ermutigt ein jungen
Bassisten, 1962.

Le pianiste de jazz
américain Dave
Brubeck (à gauche)
encourageant un
jeune bassiste, 1962.

September 1963. A photograph by George Konig of the blind American multi-instrumentalist Roland Kirk. Kirk was in London for a jazz festival.

September 1963. George Konig fotografierte den blinden, amerikanischen Multi-Instrumentalisten Roland Kirk. Kirk nahm an einem Jazz-Festival in London teil.

Septembre 1963. L'Américain Roland Kirk, multi-instrumen-tiste aveugle, photographié par George Konig. Kirk participait à un festival de jazz à Londres.

January 1962. Chet Baker, shortly after his release from prison in Rome. Baker's brillant career as a jazz trumpet player of the cool school was frequently interrupted by drugs charges.

Januar 1962. Chet Baker, kurz nach seiner Entlassung aus einem Gefängnis in Rom. Bakers glanzvolle Karriere als Jazztrompeter des Cool Jazz wurde immer wieder durch Anzeigen wegen Drogenkonsums unterbrochen.

Janvier 1962. Chet Baker, peu après sa sortie de prison à Rome. La brillante carrière du trompettiste de l'école du cool jazz fut souvent interrompue par des condamnations pour usage de drogues.

London, 1969.
Margot Fonteyn
and Rudolf Nureyev
during the final
rehearsal of a
production of the
ballet *Pelléas et
Mélisande* at the
Royal Opera House.

London, 1969.
Margot Fonteyn und
Rudolf Nurejew bei
der Generalprobe
des Balletts *Pelléas
und Mélisande* im
Royal Opera House.

Londres, 1969.
Margot Fonteyn et
Rudolf Noureïev
lors de la générale
du ballet *Pelléas et
Mélisande* au Royal
Opera House.

Luciano Pavarotti (left), Joan Sutherland and Spiro
Malas in the trio from Donizetti's opera *La Fille du
Régiment* at the Royal Opera House, London, 30
May 1966. The photograph is by Erich Auerbach.

Luciano Pavarotti (links), Joan Sutherland und Spiro
Malas in dem Terzett von Donizettis Oper *La Fille du
Régiment* im Royal Opera House, London, 30. Mai
1966. Die Aufnahme stammt von Erich Auerbach.

Luciano Pavarotti (à gauche), Joan Sutherland et Spiro
Malas dans le trio de l'opéra de Donizetti *La Fille
du régiment* au Royal Opera House, Londres, 30 mai
1966. La photo est d'Erich Auerbach.

Jack Nisberg's
striking picture of
Maria Callas,
Greek-American
opera singer, and
Aristotle Onassis,
Greek millionaire
ship owner, 1967.

Jack Nisberg machte
dieses vielsagende
Foto der griechisch-
amerikanischen
Operndiva Maria
Callas und dem
griechischen Reeder
und Multimillionär
Aristoteles Onassis,
1967.

Un portrait saisissant
de Maria Callas,
la chanteuse d'opéra
gréco-américaine,
et d'Aristote Onassis,
l'armateur million-
naire grec, réalisé
par Jack Nisberg,
1967.

February 1964.
A portrait by Erich
Auerbach of the
French composer
and conductor
Pierre Boulez.

Februar 1964.
Das Porträt des
französischen
Komponisten und
Dirigenten Pierre
Boulez stammt von
Erich Auerbach.

Février 1964. Un
portrait réalisé par
Erich Auerbach du
compositeur et chef
d'orchestre français
Pierre Boulez.

January 1962.
The English cellist
Jacqueline du Pré.
She was 17 years old
when Auerbach
took this picture,
but had already
made her debut.

Januar 1962. Die
englische Cellistin
Jacqueline du Pré.
Als Erich Auerbach
sie fotografierte, war
sie 17 Jahre alt,
doch ihr Debüt hatte
sie bereits hinter
sich.

Janvier 1962.
La violoncelliste
anglaise Jacqueline
du Pré. Elle n'avait
que 17 ans lorsque
Auerbach pris ce
cliché, mais elle
n'était déjà plus une
débutante.

June 1965.
The Russian cellist,
conductor and
composer Mstislav
Leopoldovitch
Rostropovich,
during a rehearsal.

Juni 1965.
Der russische Cellist,
Dirigent und Kom-
ponist Mstislaw
Leopoldowitsch
Rostropowitsch
während einer
Probe.

Juin 1965.
Le violoncelliste,
chef d'orchestre et
compositeur
russe Mstislav
Leopoldovitch
Rostropovich, au
cours d'une
répétition.

Igor Stravinsky
rehearses the
BBC Symphony
Orchestra, 1961.
As a composer,
Stravinsky was as
prolific as ever in
the Sixties.

Igor Strawinsky
probt mit dem
BBC Symphony
Orchestra, 1961. In
den sechziger Jahren
war Strawinsky als
Komponist so pro-
duktiv wie nie.

Igor Stravinsky fait
répéter l'Orchestre
symphonique de la
BBC, 1961. Il fut un
compositeur très
prolifique durant les
années soixante.

London, November 1963. The Russian composer Dmitri Shostakovich during a break in rehearsals of his opera *Katerina Ismailova*.

London, November 1963. Der russische Komponist Dmitrij Schostakowitsch entspannt sich während der Proben zu seiner Oper *Katerina Ismailova*.

Londres, novembre 1963. Le composi-teur russe Dimitri Chostakovitch durant une pause pendant les répéti-tions de son opéra *Katerina Ismailova*.

January 1963.
The Russian soprano
Galina Vishnevskaya
and English
composer Benjamin
Britten relax during
a recording of
Britten's *War
Requiem*.

Januar 1963.
Die russische
Sopranistin Galina
Wischnewskaya und
der englische Kom-
ponist Benjamin
Britten in einer
Pause während der
Aufnahmen zu
Brittens *War
Requiem*.

Janvier 1963.
Moment de détente
pour la soprano
russe Galina
Vishnevskaya et le
compositeur anglais
Benjamin Britten
durant l'enregist-
rement du *War
Requiem* de Britten.

6. Pop
Popmusik
La musique pop

Bob Dylan at a press reception in Britain, 3 May 1966. It was the year of Dylan's mysterious disappearance. For over three months, it was said, only the Beat poet Allen Ginsberg knew his whereabouts.

Bob Dylan auf einer Pressekonferenz in Großbritannien, 3. Mai 1966. Es war das Jahr, als Dylan spurlos verschwunden war. Nur der Beat-Lyriker Allen Ginsberg soll gewußt haben, wo er sich über drei Monate lang aufhielt.

Bob Dylan lors d'une réception pour la presse en Grande-Bretagne, 3 mai 1966. Cette année-là, Dylan disparut mystérieusement. Seul le poète beat Allen Ginsberg savait, paraît-il, où il se trouvait pendant plus de trois mois.

6. Pop
Popmusik
La musique pop

There were many who thought (and still think) that Pop was the Sixties. The roll-call of hits and stars reads like a *Who's Who* of popular music – Elvis, Ike and Tina Turner, Sonny and Cher, Little Richard, Little Eva, Buddy Holly, Hendrix, Bo Diddley, Chuck Berry, Jerry Lee Lewis, The Everly Brothers, The Doors, The Crystals, The Ronettes, The Supremes, The Animals, The Bee Gees, The Who… the list goes on for ever.

Behind all the ballyhoo, there were the starmakers – Colonel Parker, George Martin, Larry Page, Phil Spector – those who manufactured the sound or arranged the money.

Never before had music brought such fame. 'If I get any more popular,' said Eric Clapton, 'I shall have to have plastic surgery and get myself a Dr Kildare face.' Never before had record sales been so gross.

At the centre of it all were The Beatles, the four lads from Merseyside, who became the most famous people in the world. The Stones ran them close, but Mick and company were naughty and mischievous, and never straddled the generations as comfortably as John, Paul, George and Ringo. As the decade neared its end, sales of The Beatles' *Abbey Road* album topped four million in two months.

Für viele waren (und sind) die sechziger Jahre der Inbegriff der Popmusik. Die Liste der Hits und Stars liest sich wie das *Who's Who* der Musikbranche – Elvis, Ike und Tina Turner, Sonny und Cher, Little Richard, Little Eva, Buddy Holly, Hendrix, Bo Diddley, Chuck Berry, Jerry Lee Lewis, The Everly Brothers, The Doors, The Crystals, The Ronettes, The Supremes, The Animals, The Bee Gees, The Who … die Liste ließe sich noch endlos weiterführen.

Hinter dem Poprummel verbargen sich die Macher der Popstars – Colonel Parker, George Martin, Larry Page oder Phil Spector – Musikproduzenten und Manager.

Nie zuvor wurden Musiker so sehr mit Erfolg verwöhnt. „Falls ich noch bekannter werden sollte,“ erklärte Eric Clapton, „müßte ich mich wohl einer Gesichtsoperation unterziehen, um so auszusehen wie Dr. Kildare.“ Die Verkaufszahlen von Schallplatten erreichten Rekordhöhen.

Im Mittelpunkt des Popzirkus standen die Beatles, vier junge Kerle aus Merseyside, die weltberühmt wurden. Die Stones folgten ihnen knapp, doch Mick und sein Gefolge waren aufmüpfig und unbequem, und es gelang ihnen nicht, die Kluft zwischen Alt und Jung so zu überbrücken wie John, Paul, George und Ringo dies vermochten. Zum Ende des Jahrzehnts wurde das Album der Beatles *Abbey Road* innerhalb von nur zwei Monaten vier Millionen mal verkauft.

Pour beaucoup de monde, la musique pop incarne (encore et toujours) les années soixante. Du reste, les titres des tubes et les noms des stars de l'époque se lisent comme un *Who's Who* de la musique pop – Elvis, Ike et Tina Turner, Sonny et Cher, Little Richard, Little Eva, Buddy Holly, Hendrix, Bo Diddley, Chuck Berry, Jerry Lee Lewis, les Everly Brothers, les Doors, les Crystals, les Ronettes, les Supremes, les Animals, les Bee Gees, les Who … la liste est interminable.

Derrière tout ce battage, il y avait les faiseurs de stars – comme Colonel Parker, George Martin, Larry Page, Phil Spector – qui étaient aussi des producteurs de son et des faiseurs d'argent.

Jamais la musique n'avait apporté autant de gloire. « Si je deviens encore plus célèbre », déclara Eric Clapton, « il faudra que je subisse une opération esthétique pour me faire faire une tête à la Dr. Kildare. » Les ventes de disques battaient tous les records.

Au centre de ce tumulte, les Beatles, ces quatre garçons de Merseyside, atteignirent un degré de notoriété inégalé dans le monde entier. Juste après venaient les Stones mais Mick et sa bande étaient trop dépravés et débauchés pour séduire des générations entières comme John, Paul, George et Ringo surent le faire. A la fin de la décennie, la vente de l'album *Abbey Road* des Beatles avait, en deux mois, déjà dépassé les quatre millions de disques.

With his national service just finished, Elvis Presley describes how his hair was cut in the US army, 1960. He had doubts about whether he could renew his musical career.

Als Elvis Presley seinen Wehrdienst in der US-Army beendete, beschrieb er, wie man ihm dort die Haare geschnitten hatte, 1960. Er hatte Zweifel daran, ob er seine musikalische Laufbahn neu starten könnte.

Elvis Presley, qui vient de terminer son service militaire, explique comment les cheveux sont coupés à l'armée américaine, 1960. Il se demandait s'il lui serait possible de reprendre sa carrière de chanteur.

Elvis and Priscilla
Presley leave the
Baptist Hospital,
Memphis with
their baby daughter
Lisa-Marie,
10 February 1968.

Elvis und Priscilla
Presley verlassen
mit ihrer Tochter
Lisa-Marie das
Baptist Hospital
in Memphis,
10. Februar 1968.

Elvis et Priscilla
Presley quittant
l'hôpital de
Memphis avec leur
petite fille Lisa-
Marie, 10 février
1968.

A few months before he became British prime minister, Harold Wilson joins The
Beatles at the Dorchester Hotel, London, March 1964. The Fab Four were about to
be presented with the Variety Club Award as show business personalities of 1963.

Wenige Monate bevor Harold Wilson Premierminister wurde, trifft er die Beatles
im Dorchester Hotel in London, März 1964. Die Fab Four (die fabelhaften Vier)
sollten den Variety Club Award erhalten, weil sie die herausragenden Persönlich-
keiten des Showgeschäfts im Jahre 1963 gewesen waren.

Harold Wilson, quelques mois avant son élection au poste de Premier ministre, en
compagnie des Beatles au Dorchester Hotel à Londres, mars 1964. Les Fab Four
(les Quatre fabuleux) allaient recevoir le Variety Club Award (récompense) pour
leur contribution artistique en 1963.

In their early days of fame, the Beatles appear on the stage of the London Palladium, 1963. The audience numbered 2,000 screaming fans – a small gathering compared with what was to come.

In den frühen Tagen ihres Ruhms, die Beatles auf der Bühne des Londoner Palladium, 1963. Vor ihnen kreischten 2.000 begeisterte Fans – ein vergleichsweise kleines Publikum im Hinblick auf die Zukunft.

Au début de leur succès, les Beatles sur la scène du Palladium à Londres, 1963. Le public comptait 2 000 fans en délire – un petit public au vu de ce qui s'ensuivrait.

Fans attempt to break into the grounds of
Buckingham Palace as the Beatles are
presented with the Order of the British Empire
for their services to music, 26 October 1965.

Als die Beatles mit dem Orden des britischen
Königreichs für ihre muskalischen Verdienste
ausgezeichnet wurden, versuchten ihre Fans
auf das Gelände des Buckingham Palace
vorzudringen, 26. Oktober 1965.

Des fans tentent de franchir les grilles du
Palais de Buckingham durant la cérémonie au
cours de laquelle les Beatles furent décorés de
l'Ordre de l'empire britannique pour leur
contribution à la musique, 26 octobre 1965.

The Indian influence. Ravi Shankar, Indian composer and sitar
player, May 1966. As well as being George Harrison's teacher,
Ravi Shankar wrote the film score for Satyajit Ray's *Apu Sansar*.

Indischer Einfluß. Ravi Shankar, der indische Komponist und
Sitar-Spieler, Mai 1966, war nicht nur George Harrisons Lehrer,
er schrieb auch die Filmmusik zu Satyajit Ray's *Apu Sansar*.

L'influence indienne. Ravi Shankar, le compositeur et sitariste
indien, mai 1966. Shankar, qui fut le maître de George
Harrison, écrivit la musique du film de Satyajit Ray *Apu Sansar*.

The Maharishi
Mahesh Yogi instructs
John Lennon
(left foreground),
Maureen Starkey
(wife of Ringo Starr)
and George
Harrison, 1967.

Der Maharischi
Mahesh Yogi unter-
richtete John Lennon
(links im Vorder-
grund), Maureen
Starkey (Ringos Starr
Ehefrau) und George
Harrison, 1967.

Le Maharishi
Mahesh Yogi
dispense son
enseignement à John
Lennon (premier à
gauche), Maureen
Starkey (la femme de
Ringo Starr) et
George Harrison,
1967.

Horizontal…
John and Yoko in
the Amsterdam
Hilton, 27 March
1969. They spent
a honeymoon week
in bed protesting
against violence.

Horizontal … John
und Yoko im Hilton
in Amsterdam,
27. März 1969.
Während ihrer
Hochzeitsreise
blieben sie eine
Woche lang im Bett,
um gegen Gewalt zu
protestieren.

Couchés … John et
Yoko au Hilton
d'Amsterdam, 27
mars 1969. Ils
passèrent leur
semaine de lune de
miel au lit pour
protester contre la
violence.

Vertical… the famous 1968 picture of naked John and Yoko. In the Sixties, people were shocked.

Vertikal … das berühmte Foto aus dem Jahre 1968, das John und Yoko nackt zeigt. Die Menschen in den sechziger Jahren waren schockiert.

Debout … la célèbre photo de John et Yoko nus, prise en 1968. Elle fit scandale dans les années soixante.

Paul McCartney and
four-year-old Julian
Lennon, with John
in the background,
on holiday near
Athens, July 1967.

Paul McCartney und
der vierjährige Julian
Lennon, während
eines Urlaubs in der
Nähe von Athen, mit
John im Hinter-
grund, Juli 1967.

Paul McCartney
et Julian Lennon,
quatre ans, avec
John en arrière-plan,
en vacances près
d'Athènes, juillet
1967.

May 1967. Photographer Linda Eastman (later Linda McCartney) with Paul McCartney at the press launch of *Sergeant Pepper's Lonely Hearts Club Band*. The album was simultaneously released all round the world.

Mai 1967. Die Fotografin Linda Eastman (später Linda McCartney) mit Paul McCartney auf einer Pressekonferenz zu *Sergeant Pepper's Lonely Hearts Club Band*. Der Verkauf des Albums wurde gleichzeitig weltweit gestartet.

Mai 1967. La photographe Linda Eastman (plus tard Linda McCartney) avec Paul McCartney lors du lancement de *Sergeant Pepper's Lonely Hearts Club Band*. L'album sortit simultanément dans le monde entier.

Mick Jagger (left), with Stones' guitarist Keith Richards, recording music for Jean-Luc Godard's film *One Plus One*, 1968. Their notoriety had increased enormously in 1967 when they were both gaoled for possession of marijuana and four pep pills.

Mick Jagger (links) und Stones-Gitarrist Keith Richards bei den Aufnahmen zur Filmmusik von Jean-Luc Godards *Eins plus Eins*, 1968. Ihre Berühmtheit nahm noch zu, als sie 1967 wegen unerlaubten Besitzes von Marihuana und Aufputschpillen zu einer Gefängnisstrafe verurteilt wurden.

Mick Jagger (à gauche) avec le guitariste des Stones, Keith Richards, lors de l'enregistrement de la musique du film de Jean-Luc Godard *Week-end*, 1968. Leur notoriété monta en flèche en 1967, suite à leur incarcération pour possession de marijuana et de quatre pillules d'amphétamines.

Paul McCartney during the recording of the soundtrack
for *Yellow Submarine*, February 1968. The production
assistants appear less impressed than he does.

Paul McCartney während der Aufnahmen von *Yellow
Submarine*, Februar 1968. Die Aufnahmeassistentinnen
scheinen weniger überzeugt als er.

Paul McCartney pendant l'enregistrement de la bande
sonore de *Yellow Submarine*, février 1968. Les assistantes
de production semblent moins convaincues que lui.

Brian Jones, guitarist with the Rolling Stones, in concert
at the Richmond Jazz Festival, 1964. The body of Jones
was discovered in his own swimming pool in July 1969.

Brian Jones, der Gitarrist der Rolling Stones, auf dem
Jazz-Festival von Richmond, 1964. Im Juli 1969 wurde
Jones tot in seinem Swimmingpool aufgefunden.

Brian Jones, le guitariste des Rolling Stones, en
concert au festival de jazz de Richmond, 1964. Jones
fut retrouvé noyé dans sa piscine en juillet 1969.

A seething and
sweating mass
of Stones' fans at
the Wimbledon
Palais, London,
August 1964.

Die Menge der
Stones-Fans kocht
und schwitzt im
Wimbledon-Stadion,
London, August
1964.

Une foule de fans
en délire et en sueur
pendant un concert
des Stones au Palais
de Wimbledon,
Londres, août 1964.

Beauty...
Marianne Faithfull
recreates a family
portrait with her pet
dalmatian, 1964.

Die Schöne ...
Marianne Faithfull
imitiert die Pose auf
einem Familien-
porträt; an ihrer
Seite ihr Dalmatiner,
1964.

La Belle ...
Marianne Faifthfull
recompose un
tableau de famille
avec son dalmatien,
1964.

...and the Beast.
Mick Jagger at
the Regent Sound
Studio, London,
September 1964.
The public liked to
believe that Faithfull
had been corrupted
by the Stones.

... und das Biest.
Mick Jagger im
Londoner Regent-
Sound-Aufnahme-
studio, September
1964. Die Öffent-
lichkeit glaubte, daß
die Stones die Faith-
full auf die schiefe
Bahn gebracht
hätten.

... et la Bête. Mick
Jagger au Regent
Sound Studio,
Londres, septembre
1964. Le public se
plaisait à croire que
c'était les Stones qui
avaient corrompu
Faithfull.

Mick Jagger (left) and Keith Richards leave Wormwood Scrubs Gaol, London, February 1967. They had been released on bail of £7,000, following their drugs charges. The British Establishment was about to shoot itself in the foot.

Mick Jagger (links) und Keith Richards verlassen das Gefängnis Wormwood Scrubs, London, Februar 1967. Sie waren wegen Drogenbesitzes verurteilt worden, aber nach Zahlung einer Kaution von 7.000 Pfund wieder auf freien Fuß gesetzt worden. Die britische Obrigkeit hatte ein Eigentor geschossen.

Mick Jagger (à gauche) et Keith Richards quittant la prison de Wormwoods Scrubs, Londres, février 1967. Incarcérés pour usage de stupéfiants, ils furent libérés après le versement d'une caution de £ 7 000. L'autorité britannique était en train de commettre une grande gaffe.

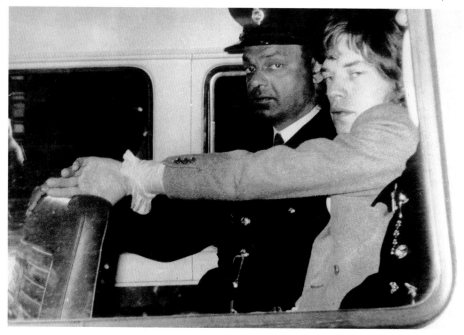

After his trial, Mick Jagger is driven to Brixton Gaol to begin a three-month prison sentence, 30 June 1967. *The Times* newspaper published an editorial the following day, headed: 'Who Breaks a Butterfly on a Wheel?' A week later, Jagger and Richards were released.

Mick Jagger wird nach seiner Verurteilung ins Brixton-Gefängnis gebracht, um dort eine dreimonatige Haftstrafe abzusitzen, 30. Juni 1967. In der *Times* stand am folgenden Tag ein Kommentar mit der Überschrift: „Wer schießt mit Kanonen auf Spatzen?" Eine Woche später wurden Jagger und Richards wieder freigelassen.

Après le procès, Mick Jagger est conduit à la prison de Brixton pour purger une peine de trois mois, 30 juin 1967. Le lendemain, le *Times* publiait un éditorial qui avait pour titre : « Le jugement n'est-il pas trop sévère pour un petit délit ? » Une semaine plus tard, Jagger et Richards étaient à nouveau libres.

The British singer
Dusty Springfield on
stage, April 1969.
She had many hits in
the Sixties, notably
'I Only Want To Be
With You' and 'You
Don't Have to Say
You Love Me'.

Die englische Sänge-
rin Dusty Springfield
bei einem Auftritt,
April 1969. Zu ihren
größten Hits in den
sechziger Jahren
zählen Titel wie:
„I Only Want To Be
With You" und „You
Don't Have to Say
You Love Me".

La chanteuse
britannique Dusty
Springfield sur
scène, avril 1969.
Un grand nombre de
ses chansons furent
des tubes dans les
années soixante,
dont « I Only Want
To Be with You » et
« You Don't Have to
Say You Love Me ».

Taking a break from
singing – Sandie
Shaw models clothes
in the window of her
London boutique,
September 1967.

Eine Auszeit vom
Gesang – Sandie
Shaw führt im
Schaufenster ihrer
Londoner Boutique
Modellkleider vor,
September, 1967.

Loin des feux de la
rampe – la chanteuse
Sandie Shaw joue au
mannequin dans la
vitrine de sa bou-
tique de Londres,
septembre 1967.

Little Stevie Wonder,
with harmonica,
March 1965.
He was 14 years
old, and beginning
to taste success.

Der junge Stevie
Wonder mit der
Mundharmonika,
März 1965. Er war
14 Jahre alt und
bereits auf dem Weg
zum Erfolg.

Le petit Stevie
Wonder avec son
harmonica, mars
1965. Agé de 14
ans, il commençait à
goûter au succès.

18 March 1965. Martha and the Vandellas in concert on the
Sound of Motown television channel. Douglas Jeffery took
this picture and the two following, all on the same day.

18. März 1965. Martha und die Vandellas bei einem Auftritt
im Fernsehkanal von *Sound of Motown*. Douglas Jeffery nahm
dieses und die beiden folgenden Fotos am gleichen Tag auf.

18 mars 1965. Participation de Martha and the Vandellas à
une audition sur la chaîne de télévision *Sound of Motown*
(célèbre maison de disques). Ce cliché et les deux suivants ont
été pris le même jour par Douglas Jeffery.

Smokey Robinson and the Miracles. The Detroit-based Motown
Corporation outsold all other American record companies in 1965, with
stars that included Marvin Gaye, the Four Tops and the Temptations.

Smokey Robinson und die Miracles. Die Plattenfirma Motown
Corporation mit Sitz in Detroit übertraf 1965 alle anderen amerikanischen Plattenfirmen, sie hatten Stars wie Marvin Gaye, die Four Tops
und die Temptations unter Vertrag.

Smokey Robinson et The Miracles. La maison de disques Motown
Corporation de Detroit, surpassa toutes ses concurrentes américaines en
1965 en produisant des stars comme Marvin Gaye, les Four Tops et les
Temptations.

Diana Ross, another *Sound of Motown* star, and lead singer of the Supremes. The group had five straight number one hits in 1964 and 1965.

Diana Ross, ein weiterer Star der *Sound of Motown* und Solosängerin der Supremes. Die Gruppe belegte 1964 und 1965 fünfmal den ersten Platz in den Charts.

Diana Ross, encore une star de *Sound of Motown*, et soliste du groupe The Supremes figura en tête du box-office grâce à cinq tubes en 1964 et 1965.

American blues
rock singer Janis
Joplin, live on stage,
1969. She died of
a drugs overdose the
following year.

Die amerikanische
Rocksängerin Janis
Joplin live auf der
Bühne, 1969. Ein
Jahr später starb sie
an einer Überdosis
Drogen.

La chanteuse de
blues américaine
Janis Joplin sur
scène, 1969. Elle
mourut d'une
overdose l'année
suivante.

Sonny (Salvatore
Bono) and Cher
(Cherilyn Sarkasian
La Pier) on honey-
moon in Britain,
August 1965.

Sonny (Salvatore
Bono) und Cher
(Cherilyn Sarkasian
La Pier) verbringen
ihre Flitterwochen in
England, August
1965.

Sonny (Salvatore
Bono) et Cher
(Cherilyn Sarkasian
La Pier) pendant
leur lune de miel en
Grande-Bretagne,
août 1965.

The American pop singer Marsha Hunt, September 1969. After famously disrobing in the stage musical *Hair* and claiming that Mick Jagger was the father of her daughter Karis, Hunt went on to become a successful novelist.

Die amerikanische Popsängerin Marsha Hunt, September 1969. Hunt machte zunächst Schlagzeilen mit ihrem berühmten Striptease auf der Bühne im Musical *Hair* und der Behauptung, daß Mick Jagger der Vater ihrer Tochter Karis sei. Später wurde sie eine erfolgreiche Schriftstellerin.

La chanteuse pop américaine Marsha Hunt, septembre 1969. Après avoir fait les gros titres en se déshabillant sur la scène du spectacle de music-hall *Hair* et en affirmant que Mick Jagger était le père de sa fille Karis, Hunt devint un écrivain couronné de succès.

Britain's finest
white soul singer,
Joe Cocker, in
mid-song at the Isle
of Wight Festival,
11 September 1969.

Englands begnadet-
ster weißer Soul-
sänger, Joe Cocker,
singt auf dem
Festival der Isle of
Wight, 11. Septem-
ber 1969.

Le meilleur des
chanteurs de soul
blancs en Grande-
Bretagne, Joe
Cocker, en concert
au festival de l'île de
Wight, 11 septembre
1969.

Pop singer David Jones, later and better known as David Bowie, 1965.
Bowie's Sixties' *Space Oddity* was notable in that he accompanied himself
with a toy Stylaphone on the hit single.

David Jones, später besser bekannt als David Bowie, 1965. Bowies Hitsingle
Space Oddity aus den sechziger Jahren ist auch bemerkenswert, weil er sich
selbst darauf mit einem Spielzeug-Stylaphon begleitet.

Le chanteur pop David Jones, plus tard mieux connu sous le nom de David
Bowie, 1965. Son tube des années soixante, *Space Oddity*, était d'autant plus
remarquable qu'il chantait en jouant sur un jouet Stylaphone pour enfant.

Marc Bolan, lead singer with T Rex, 1965. Bolan was one
of the leaders of the Glam Rock school of Pop, which
became immensely popular at the beginning of the Seventies.

Marc Bolan, Leadsänger der Popgruppe T Rex, 1965.
Bolan war eine der schillerndsten Figuren des Glam Rock,
der Anfang der siebziger Jahre enorm populär wurde.

Marc Bolan, le soliste de T Rex, 1965. Bolan était un des
chefs de file de la tendance pop glam rock qui connut un
immense succès au début des années soixante-dix.

7. Fashion
Mode
La mode

October 1965. Jean Shrimpton in
Medusa mode, displaying a 'sun' hairstyle
designed by the Parisian stylist, Carita.

Oktober 1965. Jean Shrimpton im
Medusa-Stil mit der Haarkreation
„Sonne" des Pariser Stylisten Carita.

Octobre 1965. La mode méduse illustrée
par Jean Shrimpton avec une coupe
« soleil » réalisée par le coiffeur-styliste
parisien Carita.

7. Fashion
Mode
La mode

It was as though the fashion world had suddenly discovered colour and freedom. A kaleidoscopic liberation took place after centuries of restriction. It was epitomized by the miniskirt – one small piece of material for a woman, one giant leap for womankind.

Men, too, had one of those brief periods in history when they could strut about in rich plumage. The streets of the West were thronged with dedicated followers of fashion, in Italian suits, in floral shirts, in hippie furs and flowing kaftans.

Designers and models became celebrities. People who cared little for fashion knew all about Mary Quant, Jean Shrimpton and Twiggy. Carnaby Street and the King's Road were familiar names to millions who had never been near London. The designs flowed from the drawing boards of top couturiers, and the mass-produced variations on the designs filled the rails of the chain stores and boutiques.

Some predicted that it would lead to a collapse of morals, to anarchy – or worse, to joy. The Pill and the miniskirt seemed to promise some kind of Shavian Utopia, providing the maximum of temptation with the maximum of opportunity.

It never came, but it was fun while it lasted.

Die sechziger Jahre tauchten die Modewelt in einen Rausch aus Farben. Nach Jahrhunderten der Beschränkung setzte eine kaleidoskopische Befreiung ein. Sie wurde durch den Minirock verkörpert – ein Stückchen Stoff für eine Frau, ein großer Schritt nach vorn für alle Frauen.

Auch die Männer erlebten eine kurze Epoche, in der sie sich nach Herzenslust schmücken konnten. In den Straßen der westlichen Metropolen drängten sich Modebewußte in italienischen Anzügen, Blumenhemden, Hippietüchern und wehenden Kaftanen.

Modedesigner und Models wurden zu Berühmtheiten. Selbst weniger modebegeisterte

Menschen wußten alles über Mary Quant, Jean Shrimpton und Twiggy. Die Carnaby Street und die King's Road waren Millionen vertraut, obwohl sie noch nicht einmal in der Nähe von London gewesen sind. Die neuen Kreationen entstanden am Reißbrett der großen Modeschöpfer; sie wurden tausendfach kopiert, industriell produziert und waren nun von der Stange in Kaufhäusern und in Boutiquen zu haben.

Manche phrophezeiten den Verfall der Moral und die Gefahr der Anarchie – oder schlimmer noch der Lebensfreude. Die Pille und der Minirock schienen eine Art Shaw'sche Utopie zu versprechen mit einem Maximum an Versuchungen und einem Maximum an Gelegenheiten.

Doch die bösen Vorahnungen trafen nicht ein, und man hatte eine Menge Spaß in diese Zeit.

Ce fut un peu comme si la mode avait soudain découvert la couleur et la liberté de style. Une libération kaléidoscopique se produisit, après des siècles de restrictions. La mini-jupe résume à elle seule ce phénomène. Un petit bout de tissu pour habiller une femme et un pas de géant pour les femmes en général.

Pour les hommes, ce fut aussi comme une parenthèse durant laquelle ils purent aller et venir parés comme des paons. Les rues des pays occidentaux grouillaient d'aficionados de la mode, vêtus de costumes italiens, de chemises à fleurs, de fourrures hippies et d'amples cafetans.

Les couturiers et les mannequins devinrent des célébrités. Même ceux qui s'intéressaient peu à la mode connaissaient tout de la vie de Mary Quant, de Jean Shrimpton et de Twiggy. Carnaby Street et King's Road étaient devenus familiers à des millions de gens qui n'avaient pourtant jamais mis les pieds à Londres. La mode était dessinée par les plus grands couturiers. Elle était ensuite recopiée de mille façons et produite industriellement avant de venir garnir les rayons des grands magasins et des boutiques.

Certains prédisaient que tout cela aboutirait à la fin de l'ordre moral, à l'anarchie ou, pire, au bonheur. La pilule et la mini-jupe semblaient annoncer une utopie imaginée par Bernard Shaw, alliant toutes les tentations à toutes les occasions possibles.

Aucune de ces prédictions ne se réalisa mais on s'amusa bien tout au long de l'époque.

September 1969. Yves St Laurent, flanked by two of his fashion models, Betty
Calroux (left) and Lucie de la Falaise. St Laurent opened his own fashion
house in 1962, and launched the first of his Rive Gauche boutiques in 1966.

September 1969. Yves St. Laurent mit zwei seiner Models, Betty Calroux
(links) und Lucie de la Falaise. St. Laurent gründete 1962 sein eigenes Mode-
haus und eröffnete 1966 seine erste Boutique Rive Gauche.

Septembre 1969. Yves Saint Laurent entouré de deux de ses mannequins,
Betty Calroux (à gauche) et Lucie de la Falaise. Saint Laurent créa sa
propre maison de couture en 1962 et ouvrit la première de ses boutiques,
Rive Gauche, en 1966.

The Sixties stylist.
Mary Quant arrives
at Buckingham
Palace to collect her
OBE, 15 November
1966.

Die Modeschöpferin
der sechziger Jahre.
Mary Quant bei
ihrer Ankunft am
Buckingham Palace,
wo sie für ihre Ver-
dienste im Mode-
design (OBE) aus-
gezeichnet wurde,
15. November 1966.

La styliste des
années soixante.
Mary Quant à son
arrivée au Palais de
Buckingham pour
recevoir sa décora-
tion de l'Ordre de
l'Empire britannique
(OBE), 15 novembre
1966.

The smile of the Sixties. Meagher's portrait of one of the most famous fashion models of the age, Jean Shrimpton, July 1966.

Das Lächeln der sechziger Jahre. Jean Shrimpton gehörte zu den Top-Models jener Dekade – hier von dem Fotografen Meagher aufgenommen, Juli 1966.

Le sourire des années soixante. Le portrait réalisé par Meagher d'un des mannequins les plus célèbres de cette époque, Jean Shrimpton, juillet 1966.

An icon of the
Sixties. Lesley
Hornby, better
known as Twiggy,
1967. In the
background is
boyfriend Justin
de Villeneuve.

Eine Ikone der
sechziger Jahre.
Leslie Hornby,
besser bekannt als
Twiggy, 1967. Im
Hintergrund sieht
man ihren Freund
Justin de Villeneuve.

Une icône des
années soixante.
Lesley Hornby, plus
connue sous le nom
de Twiggy, 1967.
A l'arrière-plan, son
ami Justin de
Villeneuve.

May 1966. Twiggy
stands on the back
of a car to model
a transparent plastic
halterneck dress.

Mai 1966. Twiggy
posiert auf dem
Heck eines Autos,
um ein transparentes
Trägerkleid aus
Plastik zu präsen-
tieren.

Mai 1966. Twiggy
debout sur une
voiture, vêtue d'une
robe dos nu en
plastique trans-
parent.

The scene is Chelsea. The time is August 1967. The mood is one of confidence and happiness. The boots are made for walking…

Der Schauplatz ist Chelsea im August 1967. Die Stimmung ist von Selbstvertrauen und Freude geprägt. Die Stiefel sind zum Laufen geradezu ideal …

La scène se déroule à Chelsea, en août 1967. On se sent plein d'assurance et de joie de vivre. Ces bottes sont faites pour marcher …

April 1967. A swaggering Sixties pose and a coat designed by Paco Rabanne. The coat is made of triangular pieces of leather, to look like chain-mail.

April 1967. Eine typische Pose der sechziger Jahre und ein Mantel von Paco Rabanne. Der Mantel besteht aus Lederdreiecken und erinnert an ein Kettenhemd.

Avril 1967. La pose très « sixties » se veut arrogante. Le manteau est signé Paco Rabanne et a été réalisé avec des triangles de cuir en référence à la cotte de mailles.

February 1967.
Twiggy displays one
item from a fashion
collection that she
was about to launch
in the United States.

Februar 1967.
Twiggy stellt ein
Stück aus einer
Kollektion vor, die
sie bald darauf in
den USA vertreiben
wollte.

Février 1967.
Twiggy vêtue d'un
modèle de la
collection qu'elle
s'apprêtait à lancer
aux Etats-Unis.

It was almost the mini-mac, and the hats were known as 'pork-pies'. Two nattily dressed gents step out, May 1967.

Kurze Regenmäntel und Hüte, genannt „pork-pies" (Schweinefleisch-pastete). Zwei elegant gekleidete Herren bereit, um auf die Straße zu gehen, Mai 1967.

L'imperméable dans sa version presque mini et des chapeaux surnommés « pork-pies » (pâtés en croûte). Deux jeunes gens tirés à quatre épingles prêts à sortir, mai 1967.

April 1968. Two
hippies set out on
the road to Swinging
London.

April 1968. Zwei
Hippies auf dem
Weg zum Swinging
London.

Avril 1968. Deux
hippies sur la route
du Swinging
London.

Two samples from the Spring hat collection of London designer Edward Mann, February 1966. On the left is 'Sea Diver', a vinyl helmet with a perspex earphone. On the right is 'Seaspray', a red and white racing cap with a sun-protecting visor.

Zwei Modelle aus der Frühjahrs-Hutkollektion des Londoner Designers Edward Mann, Februar 1966. Links das Modell „Sea Diver", eine Kappe aus Vinyl mit durchsichtiger Ohrmuschel aus Plastik. Rechts das Modell „Seaspray", eine steife rotweiße Kappe mit Sonnenschutzschild.

Modèles de la collection printemps de chapeaux du styliste londonien Edward Mann, février 1966. A gauche, le casque « Sea Diver » en vynile avec des oreillettes en plastique transparent. A droite, la casquette de cycliste « Sea Spray » rouge et blanche avec une visière de protection contre le soleil.

A futuristic helmet of 1966, protection against some of the mighty cold winters in the Sixties.

Ein futuristischer Helm von 1966, ideal um sich gegen die Kälte der strengen Winter in den sechziger Jahren zu schützen.

Un casque futuriste de 1966, idéal pour se protéger du froid pendant les hivers très rigoureux des années soixante.

It wasn't all miniskirt… it wasn't all clumpy platform heels. Roy Jones took this picture of a model wearing a paper dress, February 1967.

Es gab nicht nur Miniröcke … und die Schuhe hatten nicht nur klobige Absätze. Roy Jones machte dieses Foto von einem Model in einem Papierkleid, Februar 1967.

Il n'y avait pas que des minijupes … et que des grosses chaussures à semelles compensées. Roy Jones prit ce cliché d'un mannequin dans une robe de papier, février 1967.

The false eyelashes
are made from
fake flower petals
and real hair.
The lipstick, the
whole makeover, is
vintage Sixties.

Falsche Wimpern aus
künstlichen Blüten-
blättern und echtem
Haar. Der Lippen-
stift und die gesamte
Aufmachung waren
typisch für die sech-
ziger Jahre.

Les faux cils sont
faits avec des pétales
de fleur synthétiques
et de vrais cils. Le
rouge à lèvres,
comme le look, sont
typiques des années
soixante.

On the roof of
the Carlton House
Towers, London,
a model wears a
trouser suit made
entirely of white
feather boas, 1967.

Auf dem Dach des
Carlton House
Towers, London,
führt ein Model
einen Hosenanzug
aus weißen Feder-
boas vor, 1967.

Sur le toit du
Carlton House
Towers, Londres, un
mannequin porte un
tailleur entièrement
réalisé avec des
plumes de boa
blanches, 1967.

'To boldly go where no fashion designer has gone before…' A swimsuit for the space age, modelled by Judy Fairbairn, September 1969.

„Einen Weg zu gehen, den noch kein Modedesigner gegangen ist …" Das Model Judy Fairbairn stellt den Badeanzug für das Weltraumzeitalter vor, September 1969.

« S'aventurer là où aucun styliste n'a jamais osé s'aventurer … » Un maillot de bain pour l'espace porté par Judy Fairbairn, septembre 1969.

A day dress by a Milan couturier that owes much to the Op art of Bridget Riley and others, March 1966.

Ein Tageskleid, entworfen von einem Mailänder Modedesigner, bei dem der Op-Art-Stil von Bridget Riley und anderen Pate gestanden hat, März 1966.

Une robe de jour dessinée par un couturier milanais visiblement très influencé par le mouvement Op Art de Bridget Riley et d'autres, mars 1966.

The Liverpudlian singer Cilla Black models a day dress, April 1966. The marriage between fashion and pop music was consummated in the Sixties.

Die Sängerin Cilla Black aus Liverpool führt ein Tageskleid vor, April 1966. Die Verschmelzung von Popmusik und Mode war in den sechziger Jahren vollendet.

La chanteuse de Liverpool, Cilla Black, en robe de jour, avril 1966. Le mariage de la mode et de la musique pop fut consommé dans les années soixante.

2 June 1967.
For his appearance
at the West London
Magistrates Court,
Brian Jones of the
Rolling Stones wears
a boldly striped suit.

2. Juni 1967.
Brian Jones von den
Rolling Stones
erscheint vor dem
Obersten Gerichts-
hof in einem auf-
fällig gestreiften
Anzug.

2 juin 1967.
Brian Jones des
Rolling Stones, vêtu
d'un complet à
rayures tape-à l'œil,
sur le chemin du
tribunal de la Cour
de l'ouest de
Londres.

May 1968.
Trendsetters John
Lennon (left) and
Paul McCartney
arrive at Heathrow
Airport, London.

Mai 1968.
Die Trendsetter John
Lennon (links) und
Paul McCartney
treffen auf dem
Londoner Flughafen
Heathrow ein.

Mai 1968.
Les faiseurs de
mode, John Lennon
(à gauche) et Paul
McCartney, à leur
arrivée à l'aéroport
d'Heathrow,
Londres.

A pair of photographs (above and right) taken at the Biba Boutique,
Abingdon Road, London, by Stephen Archetti, July 1966. A young
woman (above) concentrates while making her selection.

Zwei Fotos (oben und rechts) aufgenommen von Stephen Archetti
in der Biba Boutique, Abingdon Road, London auf, Juli 1966.
Die junge Frau (oben) überlegt in Ruhe, bevor sie sich entscheidet.

Deux photographies (ci-dessus et à droite) prises à la boutique
Biba, Abingdon Road, Londres par Stephen Archetti, juillet 1966.
Une jeune femme (ci-dessus) réfléchit avant de faire son choix.

A woman tries on
a minidress at the
same Biba Boutique.

Eine junge Frau
probiert in derselben
Biba Boutique ein
Minikleid.

Une femme essayant
une robe courte dans
cette même boutique
Biba.

Skirting the issue. By 1969, the mini had lost some ground to the maxi, which was deemed to be equally sexy because of what it didn't reveal...

Das Problem der Rocklänge. Der Mini hatte 1969 gegen-über dem Maxi an Popularität verloren, denn nun galt jener als ebenso sexy, weil er das Verhüllte erahnen ließ ...

Le débat tourne court. En 1969, la mini avait cédé du terrain à la mode maxi, censée être tout aussi sexy car elle suggérait au lieu de dévoiler ...

...But, while the sun shone, the mini held sway. It didn't lead to a breakdown in law and order, or to rioting in the streets, though there was plenty of that about. In the end, raised hemlines led to little more than raised eyebrows.

... doch wenn die Sonne schien, wurde der Mini wieder ausgepackt. Er hatte schließlich doch nicht zu einem Verfall der Sitten geführt oder zu Aufruhr in den Straßen, Aufstände gab es wegen anderen Dingen. Am Ende hob niemand mehr die Augenbrauen wegen eines zu hohen Rocksaums.

... mais, dès que le soleil brillait, la mini-jupe était gagnante. Elle ne signifia ni la fin de l'ordre établi, ni le début de nouvelles émeutes, même si l'époque y était propice. En fait, la mode mini ne suscita que quelques froncements de sourcils réprobateurs.

8. Youth
Die Jugend
La jeunesse

To many, the Sixties were all about beauty, and that included the beauty with which, it was claimed, drugs could fill the mind. This hippie was at a pro-drugs demonstration in Hyde Park, London, 17 July 1967.

Für viele drehten sich die sechziger Jahre hauptsächlich um die Schönheit, und das beinhaltete auch jene Schönheit, mit der Drogen die Sinne erfüllten. Hier demonstriert ein Hippie für den Genuß von Drogen im Londoner Hyde Park, 17. Juli 1967.

Les années soixante riment souvent avec beauté, une beauté qui, selon certains, était aussi spirituelle grâce aux drogues. Une hippie participant à une manifestation pour la légalisation des drogues à Hyde Park, Londres, 17 juillet 1967.

8. Youth
Die Jugend
La jeunesse

When John Kennedy was elected President of the United States in November 1961, he was 43 years old. Most people regarded this as an incredibly young age to be in a position of such power. By the end of the Sixties, it seemed almost old, for the decade had witnessed young men and women, scarcely out of their teens, running revolutions, leading riots and challenging age-old authority.

Youth cut loose in the Sixties. They squatted in empty houses and smoked dope. They wore outrageous clothes. They listened to music that, even if it didn't emanate from the devil, was certainly played at a volume that suggested all hell had broken out. They fought. They danced. And worst of all, they grabbed the headlines...

They had plenty of heroes to choose from – Mary Quant, Twiggy, Jan Palach, Che Guevara, Mick Jagger, Malcolm X, Muhammad Ali, Bernadette Devlin, Danny the Red, Yuri Gagarin... DJs, pop stars, footballers, racing drivers, film stars, and the four lads from Liverpool.

But, as in all ages, most young people followed their peers – into boutiques and offices, on demonstrations and marches, to concerts and festivals.

And, at the end of the decade, the United States President was 57 years old.

Als John F. Kennedy im November 1961 ins Weiße Haus einzog, war er 43 Jahre alt. Für die meisten Menschen war damit ein unglaublich junger Mann an die Spitze einer Weltmacht getreten. Gegen Ende der sechziger Jahre schien dies wiederum sehr alt zu sein, da im Laufe dieser Dekade vornehmlich junge Männer und Frauen, kaum dem Teeniealter entschlüpft, bereits Revolutionen anzettelten, an Aufständen teilnahmen und die Autoritäten in Frage stellten.

Die Jugend befreite sich in den sechziger Jahren. Sie besetzte leerstehende Häuser und rauchte Joints. Sie trug ausgefallene Kleidung. Sie hörte Musik, die, selbst wenn sie nicht vom Teufel war, so laut gespielt wurde, daß man schließlich doch meinte, die Hölle sei ausgebrochen. Sie kämpfte. Sie tanzte. Und das Schlimmste war, sie eroberte die Titelseiten der Zeitungen …

Sie hatte genügend Helden zur Auswahl – Mary Quant, Twiggy, Jan Palach, Che Guevara, Mick Jagger, Malcolm X, Muhammad Ali, Bernadette Devlin, Danny the Red, Jurij Gagarin … DJs, Popstars, Fußballer, Rennfahrer, Filmstars und die Vier aus Liverpool.

Doch wie in jeder Epoche, schlossen sich die meisten jungen Leute ihren Altersgenossen an und folgten ihnen – in Boutiquen und ins Büro, zu Demonstrationen und Protestmärschen, auf Konzerte und Festivals.

Und am Ende des Jahrzehnts war der Präsident der Vereinigten Staaten ein Mann von 57 Jahren.

John Kennedy n'avait que 43 ans quand il fut élu président des Etats-Unis en novembre 1961. Pour une majorité de gens, il paraissait incroyablement jeune pour assumer un fonction d'une telle importance. A la fin des années soixante, il aurait semblé presque vieux car, tout au long de la décennie, on avait pu voir des filles et des garçons qui, à peine sortis de l'adolescence, avaient fait la révolution, participé à des émeutes et contesté le pouvoir en place.

Les jeunes larguèrent les amarres dans les années soixante. Ils squattèrent des maisons vides et fumèrent du shit. Ils portaient des vêtements excentriques. La musique qu'ils écoutaient n'était pas diabolique, mais était jouée si fort que le son en était infernal. Ils luttaient. Ils dansaient. Et, pire que tout, faisaient la une des journaux …

Les héros ne manquaient pas – Mary Quant, Twiggy, Jan Palach, Che Guevara, Mick Jagger, Malcolm X, Mohammed Ali, Bernadette Devlin, Danny le Rouge, Youri Gagarine … et les disc-jockeys, les stars de la musique pop, les footballeurs, les pilotes automobiles, les vedettes de cinéma et les quatre garçons de Liverpool.

Mais, comme à toutes les époques, la plupart des jeunes copiaient leurs semblables et allaient partout où les autres allaient – dans les boutiques et au bureau aux manifestations, aux concerts et autres festivals.

Toujours est-il qu'à la fin de la décennie, le président des Etats-Unis était un homme de 57 ans.

'Let's Twist again, like we did last summer...' In 1961 Chubby Checker's monotonous dance step was all the rage.

„Let's Twist again, like we did last summer ..." 1961 brachte Chubby Checker die Tanzböden mit diesem einfachen Tanzschritt zum Beben.

« Let's twist again, like we did last summer ... » En 1961, le pas de danse monotone de Chubby Checker faisait partout fureur.

September 1963.
Australian teenagers
in typical Mod
clothing, including
the classic Parker
coat, dance the
Stomp in a Sydney
club.

September 1963.
Australische Tee-
nager in der typi-
schen Kleidung der
Mods, deren klassi-
scher Parker unver-
zichtbar war, tanzen
den Swing in einer
Diskothek in Sydney.

Septembre 1963.
Jeunes australiens
habillés à la mode
des Mods, dont
l'inévitable anorak
Parker, pour danser
le swing dans une
discothèque de
Sydney.

London, June 1962. A heavenly angel in Hell's Angel garb.
The Reverend Bill Shergold (second from right) hangs out with
some of his young parishoners in the Ace Café, Hackney Wick.

London, Juni 1962. Ein himmlischer Engel in der Kluft der Hell's
Angel. Der Pastor Bill Shergold (zweiter von rechts) verbringt die Zeit
mit einigen seiner jungen Anhängern im Ace Café, Hackney Wick.

Londres, juin 1962. Un ange tombé du ciel habillé en Hell's Angel.
Le révérend Bill Shergold (deuxième à partir de la droite) boit un
verre avec ses jeunes paroissiens au Ace Café, Hackney Wick.

Mods parade along the seafront at Hastings, Sussex, 1964.
A neat appearance and a well-polished scooter were the
hallmarks of the Mod movement.

Mod-Parade auf der Seepromenade in Hastings, Sussex,
1964. Ordentliche Kleidung und ein blankgeputzer Roller
waren die Kennzeichen für Mod-Bewegung.

Défilé de Mods le long de la côte à Hastings, Sussex, 1964.
Une allure soignée et un scooter étincelant, tels étaient les
signes de reconnaissance du mouvement des Mods.

Dressed in the latest fashion, teenagers dance in a studio at the BBC
Television Centre, London, during a recording of the weekly hit music
programme *Top of the Pops*, 1967.

Angezogen nach dem letzten Schrei, tanzen Teenager in einem Studio des
BBC Television Centre, London, während einer Aufnahme des *Top of
the Pops*, eine Musiksendung, die wöchentlich ausgestrahlt wurde, 1967.

Des jeunes, habillés du dernier cri, dansent dans un studio de la BBC à
Londres, pendant l'enregistrement de l'émis-sion de variétés *Top of the
Pops*, consacrée aux tubes de la semaine, 1967.

1965, off the east
coast of England.
A DJ on the pirate
radio ship *Caroline*
is being filmed
for a documentary.

Vor der Ostküste
Englands, 1965. Ein
DJ auf dem Schiff
des Piratensenders
Caroline wird für
einen Dokumentar-
film aufgenommen.

Quelque part sur
la côte Est de
l'Angleterre, 1965.
Un disc-jockey de la
radio pirate *Caroline*
est filmé pour un
documentaire.

August 1969. Young squatters occupy an empty building in Broad Court, near Bow Street, London. Opponents of squatting regarded it at best as trespass, highly likely to involve wanton vandalism. But most squatters looked after the property that they lived in.

August 1969. Junge Leute besetzen ein leerstehendes Haus in Broad Court, in der Nähe der Bow Street in London. Gegner der Hausbesetzer betrachteten dieses Vorgehen bestenfalls als unbefugtes Betreten mit der Absicht zu mutwilligem Vandalismus. Doch die meisten Hausbesetzer hatten nicht die Absicht, etwas kaputt zu machen.

Août 1969. Jeunes squatters occupant un bâtiment vide à Broad Court, près de Bow Street, Londres. Les opposants à de telles pratiques condamnaient ces entrées non autorisées, susceptibles d'engendrer des actes de pur vandalisme. Mais la majorité des squatters respectait les lieux où ils avaient élu domicile.

The outside of
Broad Court on the
same day. Squatters
pose for Tim
Graham who took
both these photos.

Die Außenseite von
Broad Court am
selben Tag. Die
Hausbesetzer posie-
ren für Tim Graham,
der beide Aufnah-
men machte.

Broad Court vu de
l'extérieur le même
jour. Les squatters
posent pour Tim
Graham, l'auteur de
ces deux clichés.

Every era has its own drugs argot. In the Sixties, this was known as 'jacking up'. Whatever the era, the setting remains much the same – a public lavatory. This sorry scene comes from 1969.

Jede Zeit kennt ihren eigenen Drogen-Slang. In den sechziger Jahren, gab man sich einen „Schuß". Doch die Schauplätze waren zu jeder Zeit fast immer die gleichen – eine öffentliche Toilette. Diese traurige Szene spielte sich 1969 ab.

A chaque époque, son jargon des drogues. Dans les années soixante, on disait faire le cric » pour se piquer. Peu importe l'époque, le décor ne change guère – des toilettes publiques. Cette triste scène date de 1969.

All over the world, the Sixties witnessed a massive number of demonstrations to legalize the use of cannabis. Here one protestor makes his point by smoking a large reefer, 1966.

Auf der ganzen Welt gingen junge Menschen auf die Straßen, um für die Legalisierung von Cannabis zu demonstrieren. Dieser Demonstrant bringt sein Anliegen auf den Punkt, er steckt sich einen Joint an, 1966.

Durant les années soixante, il y eut partout dans le monde un nombre impressionnant de manifestations pour la légalisation du cannabis. Ce manifestant défend son point de vue en fumant un gros joint, 1966.

A member of the
Hell's Angels at the
Rolling Stones
Concert in memory
of Brian Jones,
London, 5 July 1969.

Ein Mitglied der
Hell's Angels bei
einem Rolling Stones
Konzert zum Ge-
denken an Brian
Jones, London,
5. Juli 1969.

Un Hell's Angel au
concert des Rolling
Stones dédié à la
mémoire de Brian
Jones, 5 juillet 1969.

Hippy heaven.
Two pop fans in
their finery at the
Hyde Park free
open-air concert,
20 September 1969.

Ein Paradies für
Hippies. Zwei Pop-
Fans im Hippie-
Outfit während eines
kostenlosen Open-
Air-Konzerts im
Hyde Park, 20. Sep-
tember 1969.

Le paradis des
hippies. Deux fans
de musique pop,
dans leurs plus
beaux atours, au
concert gratuit et en
plein air de Hyde
Park, 20 septembre
1969.

5 July 1969. Two members of the vast crowd
in Hyde Park dance together during the Stones
concert. Ex-Stones guitarist Brian Jones had
died just two days before the concert was given.

5. Juli 1969. Zwei Personen tanzen zusammen
in der riesigen Menschenmenge beim Rolling
Stones Konzert. Ex-Stones-Gitarrist Brian Jones
starb zwei Tage vor dem Konzert.

5 juillet 1969. Deux personnes en train de
danser parmi la grande foule réunie à Hyde
Park pour le concert des Rolling Stones. L'ex-
guitariste des Stones, Brian Jones, était décédé
deux jours avant le concert.

A small section of the half million who came to Woodstock, near Bethel, New York, on that famous day in August 1969. The fans endured traffic jams, food and water shortages, and torrential downpours to enjoy the Festival.

Einige wenige der halben Million Menschen, die zu Woodstock, in der Nähe von Bethel, New York, an diesem berühmten Augusttag 1969 gekommen waren. Sie nahmen Verkehrsstaus, Nahrungsmittel- und Wasserknappheit sowie schwere Regengüsse auf sich, um bei diesem Festival dabei zu sein.

Quelques-unes des 500 000 personnes réunies à Woodstock, près de Bethel, New York, ce fameux jour d'août 1969. Pour assister au festival, les fans avaient dû endurer les bouchons, le manque de nourriture et d'eau et des pluies torrentielles.

9. The space age
Das Weltraumzeitalter
L'ère spatiale

November 1969. A US astronaut returns to *Apollo 12* with a
container of soil from the surface of the Moon. He has a camera to
record his movements, and a check list on his left wrist. A fellow
astronaut is reflected in his faceshield.

November 1969. Ein amerikanischer Astronaut kehrt mit einem
Behälter, gefüllt mit Gesteinsproben von der Mondoberfläche, zu
Apollo 12 zurück. Eine Kamera zeichnet jede seiner Bewegungen auf,
und er hat eine Checkliste an seinem linken Handgelenk. Ein zweiter
Astronaut spiegelt sich im Visier seines Helms.

Novembre 1969. L'astronaute américain regagne *Apollo 12* avec un
tube contenant de la terre ramassée sur la surface de la lune. Il a sur
lui une caméra qui filme ses mouvements et au poignet gauche une
check-list. Dans la lunette de son casque se reflète un autre astronaute.

9. The space age
Das Weltraumzeitalter
L'ère spatiale

The billions of dollars and roubles that had been gobbled up in the space race of the Fifties at last returned a dividend. Man, and woman, conquered space. Millions of people round the world scanned the blurred images on television screens and the front pages of newspapers, and saw the first ever long-distance photographs of the Earth, and close-ups of the Moon.

It was a staggering achievement, accomplished for a mixture of good and bad reasons. There was a genuine scientific desire to find out more about our universe. There was also a squalid contest to see whether East or West would gain control of a tiny corner of the infinite.

The Soviet Union got into space first. A smiling Russian spaceman named Yuri Gagarin was the first human to follow monkeys, dogs and chickens into the great unknown. He returned to Earth a hero, to be succeeded throughout the decade by fellow citizens and by Americans. By the end of the Sixties human beings had left their footprints on the surface of the Moon.

It was a great leap for technology. By the time the *Apollo 12* mission reached the Moon near the end of 1969, the quality of the pictures transmitted back to Earth was breathtaking.

Die Millarden von Dollar und Rubeln, die in den fünziger Jahren in den Wettbewerb im Weltraum investiert worden waren, zahlten sich schließlich aus. Mann und Frau eroberten das All. Millionen von Menschen auf der ganzen Welt sahen auf ihren Fernsehbildschirmen und den Titelseiten der Zeitungen verschwommene Bilder, die ersten Fotos aus großer Distanz, die von der Erde gemacht worden sind sowie erste Großaufnahmen vom Mond.

Es war ein überwältigender Fortschritt, der aus guten und weniger guten Beweggründen unternommen worden war. Zum einen gab es ein rein wissenschaftliches Interesse, mehr über das Universum zu erfahren. Zum anderen war es ein harter Wettkampf zwischen Ost und West, um die Kontrolle über einen winzigen Raum in der Unendlichkeit des Weltalls.

Die Sowjetunion war zuerst im Weltraum. Der russische Astronaut Jurij Gagarin war der erste Mensch, der, nach Affen, Hunden und Hühnern, die unbekannten Weiten erforschte. Er kehrte als Held auf die Erde zurück, bald gefolgt von Landsmännern wie von Amerikanern. Am Ende der sechziger Jahre hatten Menschen ihre Fußspuren auf der Mondoberfläche hinterlassen.

Es war ein Meilenstein in der technologischen Entwicklung. Als die *Apollo 12*-Mission Ende 1969 den Mond erreichte, war die Qualität der übertragenen Bilder atemberaubend.

Les efforts financiers, se chiffrant en milliards de dollars et de roubles, qui avaient été engloutis dans la course de l'espace au cours des années cinquante, finirent par porter leurs fruits. L'homme et la femme conquirent l'espace. Des millions de gens à travers le monde découvrirent à la télévision ou sur la couverture de leurs journaux des images un peu floues, celles des premières photos de la Terre prises depuis l'espace et des premiers gros plans de la lune.

Cet exploit bouleversant avait été accompli pour un ensemble de bonnes et mauvaises raisons. Il y avait un réel désir scientifique d'en savoir plus sur notre univers. Mais il s'agissait aussi d'une âpre lutte que se livraient l'Est et l'Ouest pour prendre le contrôle d'un tout petit coin de l'infini.

L'Union soviétique fut la première à voyager dans l'espace et Youri Gagarine le premier cosmonaute russe à explorer le grand inconnu, après les singes, les chiens et les poulets. Il revint sur Terre en héros, bientôt suivis par d'autres Russes et par des Américains. A la fin des années soixante, des hommes avaient foulé la sol de la lune.

Ce fut un grand bond en avant pour la technologie. Quand *Apollo 12* atteignit la lune fin 1969, la qualité des images retransmises sur Terre était à couper le souffle.

April 1961.
'Flight is proceeding
normally.' Soviet
cosmonaut Major
Yuri Gagarin, who
leapt into space in
the 5,000 kg Sputnik
Vostok 1.

April 1961. „Der
Flug verläuft nor-
mal." Der sowjeti-
sche Kosmonaut
Jurij Gagarin flog
mit der 5.000 kg
schweren Weltraum-
kapsel Sputnik
Vostok 1 ins All.

Avril 1961. « Le vol
se déroule normale-
ment. » Déclaration
du cosmonaute
soviétique, le com-
mandant Youri
Gagarine, qui s'en-
vola dans l'espace à
bord du *Vostok 1,*
une fusée Spoutnik
de 5 000 kg.

May 1961.
'Everything A-OK.'
US Commander
Alan B Shepherd Jr,
second man into
space by only one
month.

Mai 1961. „An Bord
alles okay." Der US-
Kommandant Alan
B. Shepherd Jr. war
nur einen Monat
später der zweite
Mann im All.

Mai 1961. « Tout
va pour le mieux ».
Déclaration du
commandant
américain, Alan B.
Shepherd junior, le
deuxième homme de
l'espace seulement
un mois plus tard.

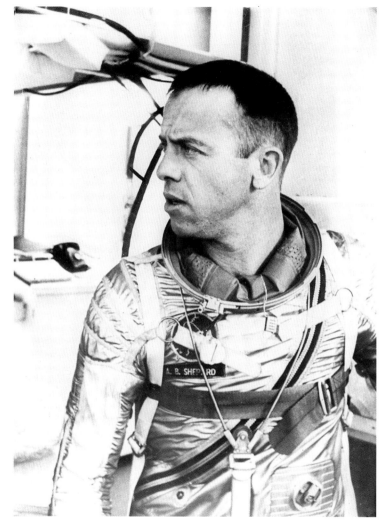

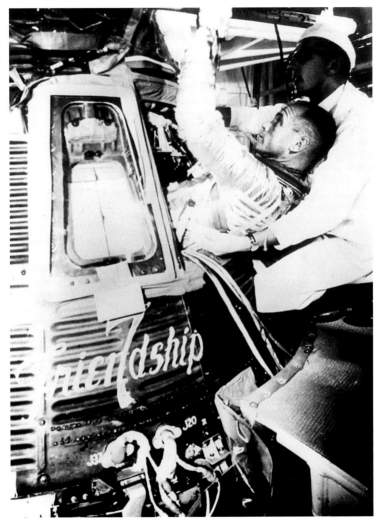

February 1962.
'Smooth and easy.'
US astronaut
Lieutenant Colonel
John Glenn and the
Friendship 7 space
capsule in which he
orbited the Earth.

Februar 1962.
„Ruhig und leicht.“
Der amerikanische
Astronaut Ober-
leutnant John Glenn
und die Weltraum-
kapsel *Friendship 7*,
in der er die Erde
umkreiste.

Février 1962. « En
douceur et facile. »
L'astronaute améri-
cain le lieutenant
John Glenn et la
capsule de la fusée
Friendship 7 dans
laquelle il resta en
orbite autour de la
Terre.

Junior Lieutenant Valentina Tereshkova, Soviet cosmonaut and the
first woman in space, practises feeding in a flight simulator, June
1963. She became a great heroine and the subject of a Russian pop
song: 'Valya, my love, you are higher than even the Kremlin...'

Unterleutnant Valentina Tereschkowa sowjetische Kosmonautin
und erste Frau im Weltraum übt die Nahrungsaufnahme in einem
Flugsimulator, Juni 1963. Sie wurde als Heldin gefeiert und ihr
wurde ein russischer Popsong gewidmet wurde: „Valya, meine
Liebe, du bist sogar noch größer als der Kreml ...“

Le jeune lieutenant Valentina Terechkova, une cosmonaute
soviétique et la première femme dans l'espace, s'entraîne à manger
dans un vol simulé, juin 1963. Elle devint une véritable héroïne et
une chanson pop russe lui fut dédiée : « Valya, mon amour, tu es
même plus grande que le Kremlin ... »

6 March 1969. In the foreground, the *Apollo 9* command module and the lunar module *Spider*. In the background, the Earth. The photograph was taken by Russell Schweickart from the porch of the *Spider* during David R Scott's space walk on the fourth day of the mission.

6. März 1969. Im Vordergrund die Kommandokapsel der *Apollo 9* und die Mondlandekapsel *Spider*. Im Hintergrund die Erde. Russell Schweickart nahm dieses Foto von der Rampe der *Spider* auf, während sich David R. Scott am vierten Tag der Mission frei im Weltraum bewegte.

6 mars 1969. Au premier plan, le module de commande *Apollo 9* et le module lunaire *Spider*. En arrière-plan, la Terre. Ce cliché fut pris par Russell Schweickart depuis l'avant du *Spider* tandis que David R. Scott faisait une sortie dans l'espace au quatrième jour de leur mission.

The *Apollo* 9 lunar module *Spider* floats upside down in space, 17 March 1969.
Inside are astronauts James McDivitt and Russell Schweickart. The module has its
landing gear deployed in what was a rehearsal for the later landing on the Moon.

Die Mondlandekapsel *Spider* von *Apollo* 9 schwebt kopfüber durchs All. An Bord
befinden sich die Astronauten James McDivitt und Russell Schweickart, 17. März
1969. Das Fahrgestell der Kapsel war ausgefahren, eine wichtige Vorraussetzung
für die spätere Mondlandung.

Le module lunaire *Spider* d'*Apollo* 9 flotte à l'envers dans l'espace, 17 mars 1969.
A l'intérieur se trouvent James McDivitt et Russell Schweickart. Le train d'atterrissage du module a été déployé pour une répétition en vue de leur futur atterrissage sur la lune.

Apollo 11 clears Launch Pad 39a at the Kennedy Space Centre, 16 July 1969. The mission to put a human being on the Moon's surface was under way.

Apollo 11 hebt von der Startrampe 39a des Kennedy-Weltraumzentrums ab, 16. Juli 1969. Die Mission, die es dem Menschen ermöglichen sollte, erstmals einen Fuß auf den Mond zu setzen, nahm ihren Lauf.

Apollo 11 franchit la rampe de lancement 39a du Centre spatial Kennedy, 16 juillet 1969. La mission qui devait permettre à l'homme de poser le pied sur la lune était en route.

'The Eagle has landed... That's one small step for man, one giant leap for mankind.' An American astronaut walks on the Moon, 21 July 1969. Neil Armstrong reported that the surface was 'fine and powdery', and that his boots sank in 'only a small fraction of an inch'.

„Der Adler ist gelandet ... Ein kleiner Schritt, aber ein Meilenstein für die Menschheit." Ein amerikanischer Astronaut spaziert auf dem Mond, 21. Juli 1969. Neil Armstrong berichtete, die Oberfläche war „fein und pudrig", und sein Stiefel „sank nur knapp einen Zentimeter in den Boden ein".

« L'Aigle s'est posé ... C'est un petit pas pour l'homme et un pas de géant pour l'humanité. » Un astronaute américain marchait sur la lune, 21 juillet 1969. Neil Armstrong déclara que le sol était « fin et poudreux » et que son pied s'enfonçait dans « moins d'un centimètre d'épaisseur ».

Neil Armstrong
stands on the Moon,
some time after
11pm, 21 July 1969.
It took over six
hours from landing
to taking the first
steps.

Neil Armstrong
betritt kurz nach
23 Uhr den Mond,
21. Juli 1969. Von
der Landung bis zu
den ersten Schritten
auf dem Planeten
vergingen sechs
Stunden.

Neil Armstrong sur
la lune peu après
23 heures, 21 juillet
1969. Plus de six
heures s'écoulèrent
entre l'atterrissage
et le moment où
l'astronaute posa le
pied sur la lune.

Richard Nixon, President of the United States, congratulates (left to right) Neil Armstrong, Michael Collins and Buzz Aldrin, on their return from the Moon, 24 July 1969. The astronauts are in a Mobile Quarantine Facility on board the USS *Hornet*, near Hawaii.

Richard Nixon, Präsident der USA, gratuliert (von links nach rechts) Neil Armstrong, Michael Collins und Buzz Aldrin nach ihrer Rückkehr vom Mond, 24. Juli 1969. Die Astronauten mußten sich zunächst in der mobilen Quarantänestation an Bord der USS *Hornet* in der Nähe von Hawaii aufhalten.

Richard Nixon, président des Etats-Unis, félicitant (de gauche à droite) Neil Armstrong, Michael Collins et Buzz Aldrin, au retour de leur voyage sur la lune, 24 juillet 1969. Les astronautes furent mis en quarantaine dans une cabine mobile à bord du navire USS *Hornet*, près d'Hawaï.

In the last days of Kennedy's presidency, an X-15 plane is launched from a USAF B-52 bomber, 16 November 1963. The X-15 reached a record altitude of 314,750 feet (97,000 metres).

In den letzten Tagen von Kennedys Präsidentschaft gelingt die Abkopplung eines USAF B-52 Bombers von einem X-15 Flugzeug, 16. November 1963. Die X-15 Maschine erreichte die Rekordhöhe von 97.000 Metern.

Quelques jours avant la fin de la présidence Kennedy, l'avion X-15 est lancé à partir du bombardier B-52 de l'armée de l'air américaine, 16 novembre 1963. Le X-15 atteignit l'altitude record de 97 000 mètres.

A mock-up of the Anglo-French supersonic passenger airliner Concorde in a hangar at Filton, near Bristol, England, 25 February 1967. The plane made its maiden flight exactly one year later, and carried its first passengers in 1969.

Ein Modell des anglo-französischen Passagierflugzeugs mit Überschallgeschwindigkeit Concorde in einem Hangar in Filton bei Bristol, England, 25. Februar 1967. Ein Jahr später machte das Flugzeug seinen Jungfernflug und 1969 beförderte die ersten Fluggäste.

Maquette du supersonique franco-anglais Concorde dans un hangar de Filton, près de Bristol, 25 février 1967. L'avion exécuta son premier vol exactement un an plus tard et transporta ses premiers passagers en 1969.

An engineer tends one of the Project Telstar communication
satellites at the Bell Telephone Laboratory, New Jersey, USA, 1963.
The work had to be done in a surgically clean environment.

Ein Ingenieur bereitet einen der Telstar-Kommunikationssatelliten
im Zentrum für Weltraumkommunikation in New Jersey, USA,
vor, 1963. Diese Arbeit mußte in einer absolut keimfreien
Umgebung verrichtet werden.

Un technicien met au point un des satellites de l'opération Telstar
au centre de télécommunications spatiales Bell Telephone de New
Jersey, Etats-Unis. Ce travail doit être effectué en milieu stérile.

A Royal Air Force officer stands at the base of the 140-foot diameter Radome, Yorkshire, England, 17 September 1963. The Radome was part of Britain's early warning system against ballistic missile attack.

Ein Mitglied der Royal Air Force steht vor dem 42,67 Meter breiten Radome in Yorkshire, England, 17. September 1963. Der Radome gehörte zu Großbritanniens Frühwarnsystem vor Angriffen mit Raketengeschossen.

Dans le Yorkshire, un officier de la Royal Air Force pose au pied du radôme de 42,67 mètres de diamètre faisant partie du programme d'alerte immédiate en cas d'attaque de missiles balistiques, 17 septembre 1963.

10. Sport
Sport
Le sport

Tommy Smith (centre) and John Carlos (right) give the Black Power
salute as the American national anthem is played at the Mexico
City Olympics, October 1968. They were subsequently suspended
for their protest against the treatment of blacks in the United
States. Peter Norman of Australia is the athlete on the left.

Tommy Smith (Mitte) und John Carlos (rechts) heben den Arm
zum Black-Power-Gruß als die amerikanische Nationalhymne bei
den Olympischen Spielen in Mexico-City ertönt, Oktober 1968.
Wegen ihres Protests gegen die Diskriminierung Schwarzer in
Amerika wurden sie von den Spielen suspendiert. Der Sportler links
ist der Australier Peter Norman.

Tommy Smith (au centre) et John Carlos (à droite) font le salut du
Black Power pendant l'hymne américain aux Jeux olympiques de
Mexico City, octobre 1968. Ils furent suspendus pour avoir
protesté contre le traitement réservé aux Noirs aux Etats-Unis.
A gauche, l'athlète australien Peter Norman.

10. Sport
Sport
Le sport

Winds of change blew through the world of sport in the Sixties, especially in Britain. The All-England Tennis Club bowed to the inevitable and admitted professionals to the Wimbledon Tournament. A year later, and with matching reluctance, cricket's ruling body abolished the distinction between amateurs ('Gentlemen') and professionals ('Players').

In March 1966 the Jules Rimet Trophy (football's World Cup) was stolen while on exhibition in London. It was found a week later in a suburban garden by a small black and white mongrel named Pickles. Honour was saved, and England won the restored Cup in July – an event from which the English have yet to recover.

Boxing took many of the headlines, with a welter of high profile heavyweight fights involving a certain Cassius Clay. He began as an amateur, winning the light-heavyweight gold medal in the Olympics at Rome in 1960. Then he turned professional and by 1964, 20 fights later, he had destroyed Sonny Liston to become world heavyweight champion. In 1965 he again floored Liston, this time as Muhammad Ali.

In between all this excitement, a very young Jack Nicklaus won his first US Masters Golf Championship.

In den sechziger Jahren wehte durch die Sportwelt ein neuer Wind, vor allem in England. The All-England Tennis Club beugte sich dem Unvermeidlichen und öffnete den Profispielern die Tore zum Tunier von Wimbledon. Ein Jahr später, und mit ähnlichem Widerwillen, hoben auch die Vorstandsmitglieder des nationalen Kricketkomitees die Unterscheidung von Amateurspielern („Gentlemen") und Profisportlern („Spielern") auf.

Im März 1966 wurde die Jules-Rimet-Trophäe (Fußballweltpokal) während einer Ausstellung in London gestohlen. Ein kleiner, schwarzweißer Hund, genannt Pickles, fand ihn eine

Woche später in einem Vorstadtgarten wieder. Die Ehre war gerettet, und England gewann den zurückgebrachten Pokal im Juli – ein Ereignis, von dem sich die Engländer heute noch erholen.

Das Boxen machte oftmals Schlagzeilen mit Kämpfen im Schwergewicht auf hohem Niveau. Im Ring stand in erster Linie ein gewisser Cassius Clay. Er begann als Amateurboxer und gewann bei der Olympiade von Rom 1960 die Goldmedaille im Mittelgewicht. Er wechselte ins Profilager und 1964, nach 20 absolvierten Kämpfen, wurde er Weltmeister im Schwergewicht, nachdem er Sonny Liston k. o. geschlagen hatte. 1965 streckte er seinen Rivalen Liston erneut zu Boden, diesmal unter dem Namen Muhammad Ali.

Inmitten all dieser Aufregung gewann der sehr junge Jack Nicklaus sein erstes US-Masters-Golfturnier.

Un vent nouveau souffla sur le monde du sport dans les années soixante, et plus particulièrement en Grande-Bretagne. La fédération de tennis All-England dut se rendre à l'inévitable et admettre la participation de professionnels au Tournoi de Wimbledon. Un an plus tard et avec autant de réserves, les responsables du cricket abolissaient la distinction faite jusqu'alors entre les joueurs amateurs (« Gentlemen ») et les professionnels (« Players »).

En mars 1966, le trophée Jules Rimet (Coupe du Monde de football) fut dérobé à Londres où il était exposé. C'est un petit chien noir et blanc nommé Pickles qui le retrouva une semaine plus tard dans un jardin de banlieue. L'honneur était sauf et, en juillet, l'Angleterre gagnait la Coupe retrouvée, un événement dont les Anglais ne se sont pas encore remis.

La boxe faisait souvent la une des journaux avec des combats de poids lourd de très haut niveau. Il y avait notamment un certain Cassius Clay. Il débuta comme amateur aux Jeux olympiques de Rome en 1960 et gagna la médaille d'or des poids moyens. Il passa ensuite professionnel et, en 1964, 20 matchs plus tard, il fut sacré champion du monde de la catégorie des poids lourds après avoir mis Sonny Liston K.-O. En 1965, il battait Liston à nouveau, cette fois sous le nom de Mohammed Ali.

Parmi toute cette agitation, il y avait le tout jeune Jack Nicklaus qui remporta son premier titre de champion au Masters américains de golf.

Goal! Geoff Hurst of England (foreground) scores the winning goal against Argentina in the quarter-final of the World Cup, 23 July 1966. Team mates include Roger Hunt (left, with arms raised) and Alan Ball (right).

Tooor! Der englische Nationalspieler Geoff Hurst (im Vordergrund) schießt im Viertelfinale der Weltmeisterschaft das entscheidende Tor gegen Argentinien, 23. Juli 1966. Zu seinen Mannschaftskollegen gehören Roger Hunt (links, mit erhobenen Armen) und Alan Ball (rechts).

But! Geoff Hurst de l'équipe d'Angleterre (au premier plan) marqua le but de la victoire contre l'Argentine en quart de finale de la Coupe du monde, 23 juillet 1966. Dans cette équipe, il y avait Roger Hunt (à gauche, les bras levés) et Alan Ball (à droite).

The Italian footballer Di Giacomo
celebrates while playing for Internazionale
against Rome, December 1962.

Der italienische Fußballer Di Giacomo von
Internazionale reißt im Spiel gegen Rom
jubelnd die Arme hoch, Dezember 1962.

Le footballeur italien Di Giacomo
de l'Internazionale au cours d'un match
contre Rome, visiblement heureux,
décembre 1962.

The last minute equalizer for West Germany in the World Cup Final,
Wembley, 30 July 1966. Wolfgang Weber (left) slips the ball past the England
goalkeeper, Gordon Banks. Then came extra time, and England's 4:2 victory.

In der letzten Spielminute fällt der Ausgleichstreffer für die Bundesrepublik
Deutschland, im Endspiel der Fußballweltmeisterschaft, Wembley, 30. Juli
1966. Wolfgang Weber (links) schiebt den Ball am englischen Torwart, Gordon
Banks, vorbei. In der Verlängerung gewann England 4:2.

Egalisation pour les Allemands de l'Ouest à la dernière minute de la finale de
la Coupe du monde, Wembley, 30 juillet 1966. Wolfgang Weber (à gauche) fait
passer la balle sous le nez du gardien de but anglais, Gordon Banks. On dut
jouer les prolongations et l'Angleterre gagna 4:2.

Wembley, 30 July 1966. England captain Bobby Moore holds the World Cup. The British press was rampant. 'If only we could see some of that ardent and united national spirit... spill over and inspire our public life,' screamed the *Daily Express*, 'then we would lick the world.'

Wembley, 30. Juli 1966. Der Kapitän der englischen Nationalelf, Bobby Moore, hält die Trophäe hoch. Die englische Presse jubelte. „Wenn nur ein Funke dieses Nationalgeistes in unser tägliches Leben überspringen würde", schrie *Daily Express*, „... könnten wir die ganze Welt besiegen."

Wembley, 30 juillet 1966. Le capitaine de l'équipe d'Angleterre, Bobby Moore, tenant la Coupe. La presse britannique se déchaîna. « Si seulement cet esprit national ardent et uni ... pouvait se répandre dans la vie publique et l'inspirer », s'écria le *Daily Express*, « alors le monde serait à nos pieds ».

1966. Gordon Banks shows his all round goalkeeper skills by catching a stray dog which had
invaded the pitch during a football match.

1966. Der Torhüter Gordan Banks zeigt, daß er
nicht nur Bälle, sondern auch einen Hund, der
während des Spiels aufs Spielfeld gelangt war,
halten kann.

1966. Le gardien de but Gordon Banks fait
une démonstration de ses multiples talents en
attrapant un chien qui s'était faufilé sur la
pelouse durant un match de football.

Eusebio (centre) is
tackled from behind
by Maldini during
the European
Cup Final between
Benefica and
Milan, Wembley,
May 1963.

Maldini foult
Eusebio (Mitte) von
hinten im Europa-
cup-Endspiel
zwischen Benefica
und Mailand, Wem-
bley, Mai 1963.

Eusebio (au centre)
est attaqué par
derrière par Maldini
pendant la finale de
la Coupe d'Europe
opposant Benefica à
Milan, Wembley, mai
1963.

Russian athlete Tamara Press creates a new Olympic
record of 59 feet 6 inches (18.14 metres) in the final
of the Women's Shot Put, Tokyo, October 1964.

Die russische Athletin Tamara Press stellt mit 18,14
Metern einen neuen Olympiarekord im Kugelstoßen
der Frauen auf, Tokio, Oktober 1964.

L'athlète russe Tamara Press bat un nouveau record
olympique lors de la finale dames du lancer du poids
avec 18,14 mètres, Tokyo, octobre 1964.

Torbjorn Yggeseth of Norway glides through the air
in the ski-jump event at the Winter Olympics,
Innsbruck, Austria, February 1964.

Der norwegische Skispringer Torbjorn Yggeseth
gleitet bei den Olympischen Winterspielen durch die
Luft, Innsbruck, Österreich, Februar 1964.

Le Norvégien Torbjorn Yggeseth glissant dans les airs
durant l'épreuve de saut à ski aux Jeux olympiques
d'hiver d'Innsbrück, Autriche, février 1964.

September 1960. The winners of Olympic medals for light-heavyweight boxing
line up on the podium at the stadium in Rome. Cassius Clay (centre), gold
medallist; Zbigniew Pietrzykowski of Poland (right), silver; Guilio Saraudi of Italy
(far left) and Anthony Madigan of Australia, joint bronze.

September 1960. Die Olympiamedaillengewinner im Leicht-Schwergewicht stellen
sich im Stadion von Rom auf dem Podium auf. Cassius Clay (Mitte) gewann Gold;
Zbigniew Pietrzykowski (rechts) aus Polen holte Silber; Guilio Saraudi aus Italien
(ganz links) und Anthony Madigan aus Australien erhielten eine Bronzemedaille.

Septembre 1960. Gagnants de la catégorie des poids moyens sur le podium du
stade de Rome. Médaille d'or pour Cassius Clay (au centre) et médaille d'argent
pour le Polonais Zbigniew Pietrzykowski (à droite). L'Italien Guilio Saraudi (tout à
gauche) et l'Australien Anthony Madigan reçurent le bronze ex-aequo.

February 1964.
After defeating
Liston, Cassius Clay
floats like a butterfly
across the ring
to urge reporters to
'eat their words'.

Februar 1964. Nach
seinem Sieg Liston,
warf Cassius Clay
sich auf die andere
Seite des Rings den
Journalisten ent-
gegen, damit sie ihre
vor dem Kampf ge-
äußerten Worte
zurücknähmen.

Février 1964. Après
sa victoire sur
Liston, Cassius Clay
bondit de l'autre
côté du ring vers les
journalistes pour
leur dire de « se la
fermer » étant donné
ce qu'ils avaient
prédit avant le
match.

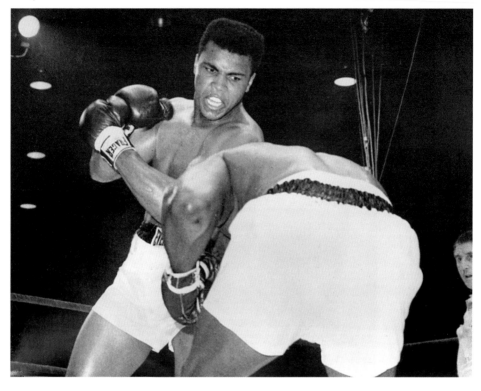

Cassius Clay in action against Sonny Liston during the Heavyweight title fight, at Miami Beach, Florida, 27 February 1964. Clay was awarded the fight when Liston failed to come out of his corner at the start of the seventh round.

Cassius Clay im Kampf gegen Sonny Liston um den Titel im Schwergewicht, Miami Beach, Florida, 27. Februar 1964. Clay siegte zu Beginn der siebten Runde, als Liston es nicht mehr schaffte, aus seiner Ecke herauszukommen.

Cassius Clay frappant Sonny Liston au cours du combat des poids lourds à Miami Beach, Floride, 27 février 1964. Clay remporta le combat au début du septième round, Liston étant incapable de se relever après le temps d'arrêt.

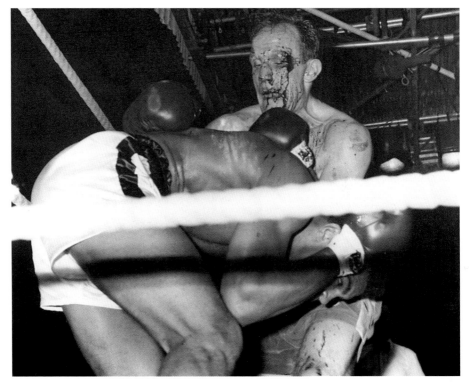

Bloodied, battered, but brave – Henry Cooper of England takes the
battle to Muhammad Ali (formerly Cassius Clay) during their title
fight in London, 21 May 1966.

Blutüberströmt, geschlagen, aber tapfer – der Engländer Henry
Cooper muß im Titelkampf gegen Muhammad Ali (ehemals
Cassius Clay) schwere Schläge einstecken, London, 21. Mai 1966.

En sang, amoché mais courageux, l'Anglais Henry Cooper continue
le combat contre Mohammed Ali (ex-Cassius Clay) lors du match
pour le titre de champion du monde à Londres, 21 mai 1966.

July 1969.
American tennis
player Billie Jean
King in action at
Wimbledon. She was
champion in 1966,
1967 and 1968,
but lost in 1969.

Juli 1969. Die ame-
rikanische Tennis-
spielerin Billie Jean
King während eines
Spiels in Wimble-
don. Sie gewann
dieses Turnier 1966,
1967 und 1968.
1969 endete die
Erfolgsserie.

Juillet 1969. La
joueuse de tennis
américaine Billie
Jean King dans le
feu de l'action à
Wimbledon. Elle
remporta le titre en
1966, 1967 et 1968
mais le perdit en
1969.

June 1962. Rod Laver of Australia successfully defends his Wimbledon title against P Darmon.

Juni 1962. Der Australier Rod Laver verteidigt in Wimbledon erfolgreich seinen Titel gegen P. Darmon.

Juin 1962. L'Australien Rod Laver défendant son titre contre P. Darmon à Wimbledon.

Winning by a nose... This award-winning sports photograph by
Reg Lancaster captures the moment when a runner hits the tape
in a novel way, 1960.

Sieg um eine Nasenlänge ... Der mit Preisen ausgezeichnete
Sportfotograf Reg Lancaster fing diesen Moment ein, als ein
Läufer auf eine neue Weise die Zielgerade passiert, 1960.

Gagné d'un nez ... Ce cliché pour lequel Reg Lancaster fut
récompensé d'un prix de la photographie sportive saisit l'instant
où le coureur touche le fil d'une manière inédite, 1960.

White City, London, 1969. The British athlete Lynn Davies stretches out in the long jump at the Amateur Athletic Association Championships.

White City, London, 1969. Der englische Athlet Lynn Davies streckt sich beim Weitsprung der Amateur-Leichtathletik-Meisterschaften.

White City, Londres, 1969. L'athlète britannique Lynn Davies saisi en plein vol pendant l'épreuve du saut en longueur au championnat d'athlétisme amateur.

December 1967.
Speed skaters in
training at Davos,
Switzerland for
the forthcoming
Winter Olympics.

Dezember 1967.
Eisschnelläufer
trainieren in Davos,
Schweiz, für die
kommenden
Olympischen
Winterspiele.

Décembre 1967.
Patineurs de vitesse
lors d'un entraîne-
ment à Davos,
Suisse, en vue des
prochains Jeux
olympiques.

August 1968. Czech diver Milena Duchkova practises in Prague for the platform diving event at the Mexico City Olympics. She took a gold.

August 1968. Die tschechische Kunstturmspringerin Milena Duchkova trainiert in Prag für die Olympischen Spiele in Mexico-City. Sie gewann eine Goldmedaille.

Août 1968. La plongeuse tchécoslovaque Milena Duchkova s'entraîne pour l'épreuve de plongée de haut vol aux Jeux olympiques de Mexico City. Elle remporta la médaille d'or.

11. Children
Kinder
Les enfants

Pre-teen Twist. Chubby Checker's 1961
dance was a hit all around the world.
It drew followers from everywhere,
including these English schoolchildren.

Twist in der Schule. Der Chubby-Checker-
Tanz von 1961 war ein weltweiter Hit.
Überall gab es Nachahmer, so wie diese
beiden englischen Schulmädchen.

Twist à l'école. Le tube de Chubby
Checker de 1961 fit le tour de la planète.
Tout le monde se mit au twist, même ces
petites écolières anglaises.

11. Children
Kinder
Les enfants

The world acknowledged the teenager in the Sixties, but tended to forget that there were still such vulnerable creatures as children. In the United States, 10-year-old girls wore bras and make-up. In Africa, 10-year-old boys (and girls) carried rifles and drilled with hastily raised militia. In China, they marched as Red Guards and carried the *Little Red Book*. In Vietnam, 10-year-olds were lucky if they survived.

Progressives and liberals campaigned for an end to corporal punishment in schools. Dr Benjamin Spock, author of *The Common Sense Book of Baby and Child Care*, became famous to some, notorious to others, because he took a stand against the Vietnam War. The book, which sold over 30 million copies, had been written in 1946, but Spock was held responsible for the subsequent flaws in an entire generation of Sixties children.

In the West there were toys in plenty, and a rapidly proliferating number of television sets. There was also more education than ever before, and more pressure to succeed. For a while it still seemed possible that parents would get what they wanted – a better life for their children, but not until those children had grown up.

And stigma still attached to illegitimate children, or even to those with divorced parents.

Die Welt erkannte in den sechziger Jahre den Teenager als Person, vergaß aber, daß es noch viel verwundbarere Wesen gab, die Kinder. In den Vereinigten Staaten trugen 10jährige Mädchen BHs und Make-up. In Afrika trugen 10jährige Jungen (und Mädchen) Gewehre und wurden vom Militär gedrillt. In China marschierten sie mit den Roten Truppen und hielten das *Kleine Rote Buch*. In Vietnam war es für 10jährige Kinder ein Glück, wenn sie überlebten.

Fortschrittliche und liberal denkende Menschen traten für die Abschaffung der Prügelstrafe in den Schulen ein. Dr. Benjamin Spocks, der Autor von *The Common Sense Book of Baby and*

Child Care, wurde berühmt, weil er sich gegen den Vietnamkrieg aussprach, einigen war er aber auch suspekt. Das Buch, das sich über 30 Millionen mal verkaufte, wurde bereits 1946 geschrieben, was niemanden davon abhielt, Spock für die Fehlentwicklungen der nachfolgenden Generation der sechziger Jahre verantwortlich zu machen.

In den westlichen Industrieländern gab es Spielsachen im Überfluß, und die Anzahl der Fernsehsender nahm rapide zu. Die Ausbildungschancen waren so gut wie nie zuvor, und der Wettbewerbsdruck stieg enorm an. Eine Zeitlang sah es danach aus, als würde sich der Wunsch vieler Eltern erfüllen – ein besseres Leben für ihre Kinder, aber ohne aus ihnen verwöhnte Erwachsene machen zu wollen.

Auf uneheliche Kinder oder Kinder von geschiedenen Eltern wurde immer noch mit dem Finger gezeigt.

Les années soixante furent marquées par la reconnaissance de l'adolescent en tant que personne, mais oublièrent qu'il existait encore des êtres très vulnérables, les enfants. Alors qu'aux Etats-Unis des petites filles de 10 ans portaient un soutient-gorge et se maquillaient. En Afrique des garçons (et des filles) du même âge portaient des fusils et s'entraînaient aux côtés de miliciens de fortune. En Chine, ils défilaient avec les Gardes Rouges, tout en tenant le *Petit Livre rouge*. Au Viêt-nam, c'était une chance si les enfants de 10 ans étaient encore en vie.

Les progressistes et les libéraux s'étaient mis en campagne contre la punition corporelle à l'école. Le Dr. Benjamin Spock, auteur de *Common Sense Book of Baby and Child Care* (*Comment soigner et éduquer son enfant*), devint célèbre pour ses critiques de la guerre du Viêt-nam. Certains affirmèrent qu'il profita de cette cause pour se faire connaître. Son livre, vendu à plus de 30 millions d'exemplaires, avait été écrit en 1946, et pourtant Spock fut tenu pour responsable de tous les défauts de la génération des enfants des années soixante.

A l'Ouest, il y avait des jouets en abondance et toujours plus de postes de télévision. L'éducation était plus accessible que jamais et la pression pour réussir à l'école toujours plus grande. Ce fut une époque où il semblait possible pour les parents d'obtenir ce qu'ils souhaitaient – une meilleure vie pour leurs enfants, sans en faire des adolescents gâtés pour autant.

Quant aux enfants illégitimes, ils étaient encore montrés du doigt, tout comme les enfants de parents divorcés.

December 1960. The Oliver Twist of the Sixties.
A young boy tucks into his Christmas dinner at a party
held for orphans and children of broken marriages.

Dezember 1960. Der Oliver Twist der sechziger Jahre.
Auf einer Weihnachtsfeier für Waisen und Kinder aus
zerrütteten Ehen verschlingt ein kleiner Junge sein
Weihnachtsessen.

Décembre 1960. L'Oliver Twist des années soixante. Un
petit garçon engloutit son repas de Noël à une fête donnée
pour les orphelins et les enfants de parents divorcés.

Two young American boys enjoy hot dogs
during a baseball match, 1960. To be young
(and wealthy) in the United States was definitely
where it was at.

Zwei amerikanische Jungen verspeisen bei
einem Baseball-Spiel ihre Hot Dogs. Amerika
war das Land um jung (und reich) zu sein, 1960.

Deux petits Américains dégustent leur hot-dog
durant un match de base-ball, 1960. Etre jeune
(et riche) aux Etats-Unis, c'était ça l'idéal.

A primary-school child demonstrates the 'Initial Teaching Alphabet', 1961. In Britain this phonetically based scheme was used in experiments to teach reading.

Eine Erstklässerin demonstriert das „Initial Teaching Alphabet", 1961. Das auf Phonetik basierende Schema wurde in Großbritannien im Leseunterricht ausprobiert.

Elève d'une école primaire en train d'apprendre l'alphabet avec « Initial Teaching Alphabet », 1961. En Grande-Bretagne, cette méthode, qui reposait sur la phonétique, était expérimentée pour l'apprentissage de la lecture.

A ballroom dancing lesson at the Holmshill Secondary School at Boreham Wood, Hertfordshire, January 1960. As a social skill the importance of ballroom dancing was declining in favour of twisting, jiving, and rockin' and rollin'.

Tanzstunde im Gymnasium von Holmshill in Boreham Wood, Hertfordshire, Januar 1960. Das Erlernen von Gesellschaftstänzen gehörte mit zum Pflicht-programm für junge Menschen, doch Twist, Jive und Rock 'n' Roll verdrängten die Standardtänze.

Leçon de danse de salon à l'école secondaire de Holmshill à Boreham Wood, Hertfordshire, Angleterre, janvier 1960. La danse de salon en tant que qualité sociale passait de mode au profit du twist, du swing et du rock'n roll.

All mucked up... the perennial joys of the custard-pie
routine. These children, however, are covered in the
remains of a sticky bun fight, January 1967.

Ganz schön bekleckert ... die alljährliche Freude von
Sahnetorten. Diese Kinder tragen die jedoch süßen Spuren
einer Kuchenschlacht am ganzen Körper, Januar 1967.

Sales de la tête au pied ... les éternelles joies de la tarte
à la crème. En l'occurrence, ces enfants portent les traces
d'une bataille de gateaux, janvier 1967.

All cleaned up… Allen and Neil Dockerty polish boots on the streets of Ashington, Northumberland, August 1961. They were helping to raise money for a new Boys' Brigade headquarters in London.

Ganz schön sauber … Allen und Neil Dockerty betätigen sich in den Straßen von Ashington, Northumberland, als Schuhputzer, August 1961. Ihre Einnahmen kamen der neuen Zentralstelle einer Jungengruppe in London zugute.

Propres de la tête au pied … Allen et Neil Dockerty cirent des chaussures dans une rue d'Ashington, Northumberland, août 1961. Ils participaient ainsi à la collecte de fonds pour la construction d'un nouveau bâtiment pour les scouts à Londres.

A boy dressed as a cowboy rides through Wenceslas Square, Prague, during the traditional St Matthew Fair, 25 February 1969. Six months earlier, the square had been full of Russian tanks.

Ein kleiner Junge, als Cowboy verkleidet, reitet über den Wenzelsplatz beim traditionellen St.-Matthew-Markt, 25. Februar 1969. Noch ein halbes Jahr zuvor war der Platz mit russischen Panzern übersät.

Un garçon habillé en cow-boy traverse à cheval la place Wenceslas à Prague durant la traditionnelle foire de Saint-Mathieu, 25 février 1969. Six mois plus tôt, la place était couverte de chars russes.

In Moon-landing mode. A young would-be astronaut celebrates an historic achievement.

Das richtige Outfit für die Mondlandung. Ein junger Möchtegern-Astronaut feiert ein historisches Ereignis.

Habillé pour aller sur la lune. Un astronaute en herbe célèbre à sa manière un événement historique.

Crystal Palace race track, London, June 1967. The next generation of Graham Hills, Jackie Stewarts, and Nigel Mansells? Young drivers line up on the grid for the start of a pedal car Junior Grand Prix.

Crystal-Palace-Rennstrecke, London, Juni 1967. Die nächste Generation der Graham Hills, Jackie Stewarts und Nigel Mansells? Junge Fahrer an der Startlinie in ihrem Tretauto beim Junior Grand Prix.

Course automobile au Crystal Palace, Londres, juin 1967. Est-ce la nouvelle génération des Graham Hill, Jackie Stewart et Nigel Mansell ? Les jeunes coureurs se mettent en position sur la grille de départ du Grand Prix Junior de la voiture à pédales.

Without the aid of Robin, Batman (alias Adam West) helps a
group of London children cross the road safely in Kensington,
May 1967. The stunt was part of a road safety film.

Batman (alias Adam West) führt, ohne die Hilfe von Robin
eine Gruppe Schulkinder sicher über eine Straße in Kensington, Mai 1967. Die Szene stammt aus einem Film zu mehr
Sicherheit im Straßenverkehr.

Sans l'aide de Robin, Batman (alias Adam West) aide un groupe
de petits Londoniens à traverser la rue en toute sécurité,
Kensington, mai 1967. Il s'agissait en fait d'une mise en scène
pour un film de la prévention routière.

Local children from Crystal Palace, London, parade to show the number of fatal road accidents, May 1964. The parade was held as part of 'Think Ahead', the National Road Safety Campaign.

Kinder aus Crystal Palace, London haben sich zu der Zahl formiert, die die Höhe der tödlichen Verkehrsunfälle angibt, Mai 1964. Diese Demonstration war Teil der Kampagne „Denk' im Voraus!" zur Sicherheit auf öffentlichen Straßen.

Des enfants du quartier du Crystal Palace, Londres, défilent en formant le nombre de victimes d'accidents de la route, mai 1964. Cette manifestation faisait partie de la campagne « Mieux vaut prévenir » de la Sécurité routière nationale.

Schoolchildren
practise road safety
in the playground,
November 1962.
The Sixties saw a
vast increase in the
number of vehicles
on the road.

Schulkinder üben
das Verhalten im
Straßenverkehr auf
dem Pausenhof,
November 1962. In
den sechziger Jahren
war das Verkehrsauf-
kommen sprunghaft
angestiegen.

Des écoliers s'ini-
tient à la sécurité
routière dans la
cour de leur école,
novembre 1962. Au
cours des années
soixante, le nombre
de véhicules sur la
route augmenta
considérablement.

Patriotic headgear, 1968. A young child on her way to a party organized by the League of Pity at the Hyde Park Hotel, London.

Ein patriotischer Kopfschmuck, 1968. Das kleine Mädchen ist auf dem Weg zu einer Wohltätigkeitsveranstaltung der League of Pity im Hyde Park Hotel, London.

Chapeau patriotique, 1968. Cette petite fille s'apprête à participer à une fête de la League of Pity (charité pour les pauvres) au Hyde Park Hotel, Londres.

6 August 1962. A young boy holds the national flag at celebrations to mark the independence of Jamaica.

6. August 1962. Ein kleiner Junge hält bei den Straßenfeierlichkeiten zur Unabhängigkeit Jamaikas die Flagge seines Landes in der Hand.

6 août 1962. Ce petit garçon tient un drapeau national pendant les célébrations marquant l'indépendance de la Jamaïque.

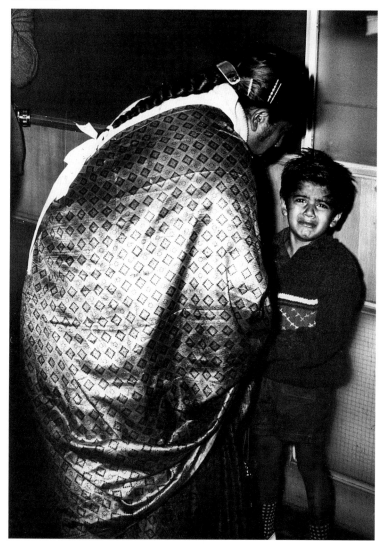

Newcomers from
the East. An Asian
mother and child
arrive at London's
Heathrow Airport,
1968.

Neuankömmlinge
aus dem Osten. Eine
asiatische Mutter
kommt mit ihrem
Kind auf dem
Londoner Flughafen
Heathrow an, 1968.

Nouveaux venus
en provenance de
l'Est. Arrivée d'une
mère et d'un enfant
asiatiques à l'aéro-
port de Heathrow,
Londres, 1968.

Newcomers from the West. Two children arrive in Britain by boat from the Caribbean, June 1962. The steady increase in the number of immigrants was exploited by some racist British politicians.

Neuankömmlinge aus dem Westen. Die beiden Kinder kamen mit dem Schiff aus der Karibik nach England, Juni 1962. Die ständig wachsende Zahl von Einwanderern nutzten einige rassistische Politiker für ihre Wahlkampfzwecke.

Nouveaux venus en provenance de l'Ouest. Arrivée par bateau en Grande-Bretagne de deux enfants des Caraïbes, juin 1962. L'augmentation régulière du nombre des immigrés fut exploitée par certains politiciens britanniques racistes.

Chinese girls, armed
with sub-machine
guns, march in
Peking to celebrate
Youth and Vigour
Day, 1960.

Chinesische Mäd-
chen mit Maschinen-
gewehren bei einer
Parade, um den Tag
der Jugend und
Kraft zu feiern.

Jeunes filles
chinoises, armées
d'une mitraillette,
participant à un
défilé pour célébrer
la journée de la
jeunesse et de la
vigueur à Pékin,
1960.

A very young Mau
Mau forest fighter,
20 December 1963.
The picture was
taken just eight days
after Kenya's
independence.

Ein sehr junger
Mau-Mau-Dschun-
gelkämpfer, 20. De-
zember 1963. Das
Foto wurde nur acht
Tage nach Kenias
Unabhängigkeit
aufgenommen.

Un très jeune
combattant du
maquis Mau-Mau,
20 décembre 1963.
Ce cliché fut pris
une semaine
seulement après
l'indépendance du
Kenya.

Joan Collins and
her daughter, Tara,
November 1968.
Tara was rehearsing
Airs and Graces
at the Scala Theatre,
London.

Joan Collins mit
ihrer Tochter Tara,
November 1968.
Tara probte für die
Aufführung *Airs and
Graces* im Londoner
Scala Theatre.

Joan Collins et sa
fille Tara, novembre
1968. Tara répétait
Airs and Graces au
Scala Theatre,
Londres.

December 1968. John Winston Lennon of Beatles fame, and
his son Julian, in the last great decade of the fur coat. Lennon's
marriage to his first wife, Cynthia, had broken up. Three
months later he married Yoko Ono.

Dezember 1968. John Winston Lennon von den Beatles und
sein Sohn Julian in den letzten Tagen der Fellmäntel. Die Ehe
mit Lennons erster Frau Cynthia war in die Brüche gegangen.
Drei Monate später heiratete er Yoko Ono.

Décembre 1968. John Winston Lennon, connu comme un des
Beatles, et son fils Julian à la grande (et dernière) époque du
manteau de fourrure. Lennon venait de rompre avec sa première
femme, Cynthia. Trois mois plus tard, il épousait Yoko Ono.

June 1962. Frank Sinatra, American singer and
film actor, at a home for blind children in
Northwood, Middlesex, during a visit to Britain.

Juni 1962. Während eines Englandaufenhalts
besucht der amerikanische Sänger und Schauspieler Frank Sinatra ein Heim für blinde Kinder
in Northwood, Middlesex.

Juin 1962. Frank Sinatra, le chanteur et acteur
américain, dans un foyer pour enfants aveugles à
Northwood, Middlesex, lors d'un voyage en
Grande-Bretagne.

One of the hundreds of victims of the drug thalidomide, a child at a nursery in Cologne, Germany, is fitted with new arms, April 1967.

Ein kleines Mädchen, das zu den Hunderten von Contergan-Opfern zählt, bekommt in einer Kölner Kindertagesstätte Armprothesen angelegt, April 1967.

Une des centaines de victimes du médicament Thalidomide. Dans une garderie de Cologne, Allemagne, cette petite fille est équipée de nouveaux bras, avril 1967.

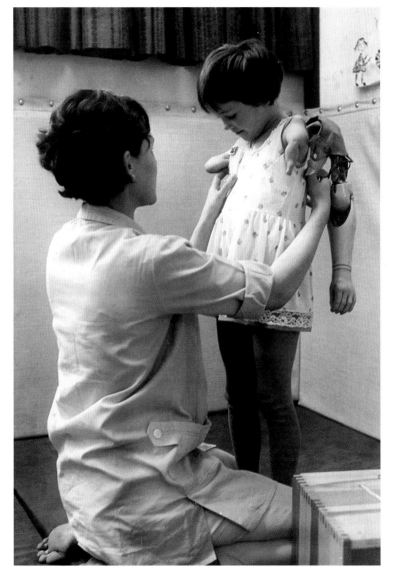

Lady Di aged six.
Diana Frances
Spencer with her
brother Charles,
at Sandringham,
July 1967.

Lady Di im Alter
von sechs Jahren.
Diana Frances
Spencer mit ihrem
Bruder Charles
auf dem Anwesen
Sandringham,
Juli 1967.

Lady Di à l'âge de
six ans. Diana
Frances Spencer avec
son frère Charles à
Sandrigham, juillet
1967.

Prince Charles aged eleven. The young prince is at the Badminton Horse Trials on the Duke of Beaufort's Gloucestershire estate, April 1960.

Prinz Charles mit elf Jahren. Der junge Prinz besucht das Pferderennen von Badminton auf dem Gelände des Herzogs von Beaufort in Gloucestershire, April 1960.

Le Prince Charles à l'âge de onze ans. Le jeune prince au concours hippique de Badminton qui se déroulait sur la propriété du duc de Beaufort dans le Gloucestershire, avril 1960.

12. Guilt and grief
Schuldgefühle und Trauer
Remords et chagrins

Members of the Kennedy family at John Kennedy's funeral,
25 November 1963. (From left, back row) Senator Edward Kennedy,
Jackie Kennedy and Robert Kennedy. (Foreground) Kennedy's two
children – Caroline (aged 6) and John (aged 3).

Die Mitglieder der Kennedy-Familie während der Begräbnisfeier von
John Kennedy, 25. November 1963. (Von links, hintere Reihe) Senator
Edward Kennedy, Jackie Kennedy und Robert Kennedy. (Im Vordergrund)
die beiden Kinder Kennedys – Caroline (6 Jahre) und John (3 Jahre).

Membres de la famille Kennedy aux funérailles de John Kennedy,
25 novembre 1963. (De gauche à droite, au 2ᵉ rang) le sénateur Edward
Kennedy, Jackie Kennedy et Robert Kennedy. (Au premier plan) les deux
enfants de Kennedy – Caroline (6 ans) et John (3 ans).

12. Guilt and grief
Schuldgefühle und Trauer
Remords et chagrins

In any decade enough harm is done by human beings, but nature also takes a killing hand. In the Sixties there were fires in California and floods in Florence. Three thousand people were killed in a landslide in Peru and there was an appalling earthquake in Skopje, Yugoslavia.

Alongside these disasters there were grim accidents. In the early Sixties hundreds were killed in a succession of plane crashes, at Orly, New York City, and Guam. In December 1963, 159 people perished in a fire on the Greek liner *Lakonia*. Astronauts Grissom, White and Clark became the first Americans to die in the space race when their *Apollo 1* spaceship exploded in January 1967. Over 300 Peruvian football fans were crushed to death in a crowd stampede in May 1964.

But the tragedies that made the biggest headlines were neither acts of nature nor accidents. There were individual assassinations, and mass killings. Richard F Speck killed eight nurses in Chicago in 1966. Charles J Whitman gunned down twelve students at the University of Texas one August afternoon in the same year. Charles Manson and followers perpetrated their massacre in 1969. The Moors Murderers, Hindley and Brady were finally arrested in 1965.

The Swinging Sixties had their dark side.

Jedes Jahrzehnt kennt seine von Menschenhand provozierten Tragödien, aber ebenso geschieht es, daß die Natur zuschlägt. In den sechziger Jahren gab es Großbrände in Kalifornien und Überschwemmungen in Florenz. 3.000 Menschen kamen bei einem Erdrutsch in Peru ums Leben und die ehemalige jugoslawische Stadt Skopje wurde von einem Erdbeben heimgesucht.

Neben diesen Naturkatastrophen versetzten tragische Unfälle die Menschen in Angst und Schrecken. Anfang der sechziger Jahre starben Hunderte von Menschen bei Flugzeugabstürzen in Orly, New York City und Guam. Im Dezember 1963 fanden 159 Menschen in den Flammen auf dem griechischen Linienschiff *Lakonia* den Tod. Die Astronauten Grissom, White und Clark waren die ersten Amerikaner, die im Rennen um den Weltraum zu Tode kamen, als die *Apollo 1* im Januar 1967 explodierte. Im Mai 1964 wurden in Peru über 300 Fußballfans zu Tode getrampelt.

Doch die Schlagzeilen, die für das größte Aufsehen sorgten, waren weder Naturkatastrophen noch Unfälle. Es handelte sich vielmehr um Einzelmorde und Massentötungen. Richard F. Speck brachte 1966 in Chicago acht Krankenschwestern um. Charles J. Whitman schoß an einem Nachmittag im August desselben Jahres auf dem Gelände der Universität von Texas zwölf Studenten nieder. Charles Manson und seine Anhänger richteten 1969 ein Massaker an. Die Mörder aus dem Moor, Hindley und Brady, wurden 1965 endlich festgenommen.

Die Swinging Sixties hatten auch ihre Schattenseiten.

Chaque décennie connaît son lot de tragédies causées par l'homme mais il arrive que la nature frappe elle aussi. Dans les années soixante, il y eut des incendies en Californie et des inondations à Florence. Au Pérou, un glissement de terrain causa la mort de 3 000 personnes. En Yougoslavie, un tremblement de terre ravagea la ville de Skopje.

A ces catastrophes naturelles s'ajouta une série d'accidents tragiques. Au début des années soixante, des centaines de personnes moururent dans des accidents d'avion à Orly, New York et Guam. En décembre 1963, 159 personnes périrent dans l'incendie du paquebot grec, le *Lakonia*. En janvier 1967, la fusée *Apollo 1* explosa en vol, faisant des astronautes Grissom, White et Clark les premières victimes de la course à l'espace. En mai 1964, plus de 300 supporters de football péruviens furent piétinés à mort par la foule.

Mais les tragédies qui firent les plus grands titres n'étaient ni des catastrophes naturelles, ni des accidents. Il s'agissait d'assassinats individuels ou des meurtres en série. En 1966, Richard F. Speck tua huit infirmières à Chicago. Charles J. Whitman tira sur douze étudiants de l'Université du Texas un après-midi d'août de la même année. Charles Manson et ses adeptes perpétrèrent leur massacre en 1969. Les assassins des landes, Hindley et Brady, furent enfin arrêtés en 1965.

Les swinging sixties connurent aussi des heures sombres.

23 October 1966. The Aberfan disaster,
South Wales. 144 people died, nearly all
of them children, when a slag heap
collapsed and two million tons of mine
waste engulfed the Pantglas Infants and
Junior School at 9.30 in the morning, as
the children gathered for assembly.

23. Oktober 1966. Das Aberfan-Unglück,
Südwales. Ein riesiger Schlammberg brach
um 9.30 Uhr in sich zusammen und riß
tonnenweise Minenabfälle mit sich. Die
Erdmassen begruben 144 Menschen unter
sich, hauptsächlich Kinder, die sich vor der
Grundschule versammelt hatten.

23 octobre 1966. Le désastre d'Aberfan
au sud du Pays de Galles. 144 personnes
périrent, presque tous des enfants, après
l'effondrement d'une masse de terril. Deux
millions de tonnes de charbon engloutirent
l'école maternelle et primaire de Pantglas
à 9h30 du matin alors que les enfants
venaient de se réunir dans le hall central.

Mrs Ann Downey watches police search Saddleworth Moors for the body of her daughter Lesley, October 1965. Lesley Downey was one of the victims of Myra Hindley and Ian Brady, who became perhaps the most hated killers in British history.

Ann Downey ist bei der Suchaktion nach dem Leichnam ihrer Tochter Lesley der Polizei im Moor von Saddelworth anwesend, Oktober 1965. Lesley Downey war eines der Opfer, die Myra Hindley und Ian Brady, die wahrscheinlich die meistgehaßten Mörder in der britischen Kriminalgeschichte wurden.

Mme Ann Downey assiste aux recherches menées par la police dans les landes de Saddleworth pour retrouver le corps de sa fille Lesley, octobre 1965. Lesley fut une des victimes de Myra Hindley et Ian Brady, peut-être les criminels les plus haïs de l'histoire britannique.

Ian Brady on his way to make his first court appearance, 22 October 1965. Unlike Hindley, Brady later expressed a wish never to be released from gaol.

Ian Brady auf dem Weg, dem obersten Richter vorgeführt zu werden, 22. Oktober 1965. Im Gegensatz zu Hindley, erklärte Brady später, daß es besser sei, wenn er zeitlebens im Gefängnis bliebe.

Ian Brady en route pour sa première séance au tribunal, 22 octobre 1965. Contrairement à Hindley, Brady demanda par la suite à n'être jamais libéré de prison.

Tears for Marilyn.
Joe DiMaggio,
Monroe's second
husband, weeps at
her graveside, 1962.

Tränen für Marilyn.
Joe DiMaggio,
Monroes zweiter
Ehemann, weint an
ihrem Grab, 1962.

Larmes pour
Marilyn. Joe
DiMaggio, le
deuxième époux de
Monroe, pleure sur
sa tombe, 1962.

Death of a legend.
Medical attendants
remove the body of
Marilyn Monroe
from her home,
9 August 1962.

Tod einer Legende.
Sanitäter bringen
den Leichnam von
Marilyn Monroe
aus ihrem Haus,
9. August 1962.

La mort d'une
légende. Des infir-
miers emmènent le
corps de Marilyn
Monroe, 9 août
1962.

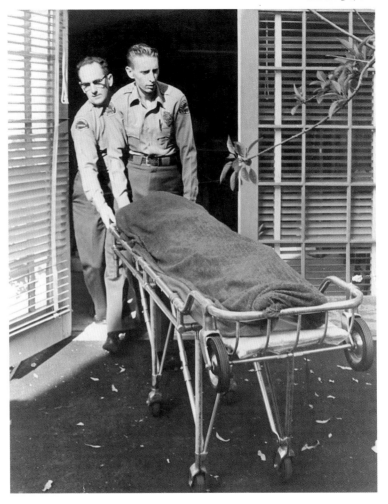

The end of a failing career. The wreckage of the car in which
Hollywood star and sex symbol Jayne Mansfield was killed,
29 June 1967. The car collided with a lorry near New Orleans.

Das Ende einer gescheiterten Karriere. Das Autowrack, in dem
der Hollywood-Star und das Sexsymbol Jayne Mansfield töd-
lich verunglückte, 29. Juni 1967. Der Wagen war in der Nähe
von New Orleans mit einem Laster zusammengeprallt.

La fin d'une carrière ratée. Décombres de la voiture dans
laquelle Jayne Mansfield, star et sex-symbol d'Hollywood,
trouva la mort le 29 juin 1967 à la suite d'une collision avec
un camion près de la Nouvelle-Orléans.

'You wreck 'em, we fetch 'em'. Senator Edward Kennedy's car is recovered from the water near Chappaquiddick Island, Massachusetts, 19 July 1969. Inside is the body of Mary Jo Kopechne, who died when the car, driven by Kennedy, plunged over a bridge. Thus ended a promising career.

„Sie fahren sie kaputt, wir bergen sie". Der Wagen von Senator Edward Kennedy wird in der Nähe der Insel Chappaquiddick, Massachusetts, aus dem Wasser geborgen, 19. Juli 1969. Im Wagen fand man den Leichnam von Mary Jo Kopechne. Sie starb, als das Auto, das Kennedy lenkte, von der Brücke stürzte. Das Ende einer vielversprechenden Karriere.

« Si ça casse, on passe. » La voiture du sénateur Edward Kennedy fut repêchée près de l'île de Chappaquiddick, Massachusetts, 19 juillet 1969. A l'intérieur gisait le corps de Mary Jo Kopechne qui fut tuée lorsque la voiture, conduite par Kennedy, culbuta par-dessus le pont. La fin d'une carrière prometteuse.

Christine Keeler leaves court, 22 July 1963. A model and showgirl, her part in the Profumo Affair helped bring down the British Government.

Christine Keeler verläßt den Gerichts-saal, 22. Juli 1963. Die Aussagen des Fotomodells und Showgirls in der Profumo-Affäre trugen zum Sturz der britischen Regierung bei.

Christine Keeler à sa sortie du tribunal, 22 juillet 1963. Mannequin et séductrice, son rôle joué dans le scandale Profumo contribua à faire chuter le gouvernement britannique.

July 1963. Mandy
Rice-Davies (centre,
right) and Christine
Keeler leave the Old
Bailey. It was alleged
that War Minister
John Profumo had
shared the favours of
Keeler with a Soviet
naval attaché.

Juli 1963. Mandy
Rice-Davies (Mitte,
rechts) und Christine
Keeler verlassen den
Obersten Strafge-
richtshof. Verteidi-
gungsminister John
Profumo soll Keelers
Gunst mit einem so-
wjetischen Marine-
attaché geteilt
haben.

Juillet 1963. Mandy
Rice-Davies (au
centre, à droite) et
Christine Keeler
quittant la cour
d'assises de Londres.
Le ministre de la
Défense, John
Profumo, était
accusé d'avoir par-
tagé les faveurs de
Keeler avec un
attaché de la marine
soviétique.

August 1963. Three of the suspects in the Great Train Robbery leave Linslade Court, Buckinghamshire. The gang got away with £2.5 million when they held up the overnight Glasgow-to-London Royal Mail train.

August 1963. Drei der Verdächtigen des spektakulären Zugüberfalls werden aus dem Gerichtshof von Linslade in Buckinghamshire geführt. Die Bande erbeutete bei dem Überfall auf den Postzug von Glasgow nach London 2,5 Millionen Pfund.

Août 1963. Trois des suspects du vol du Londres-Glasgow quittant le tribunal de Linslade, Buckinghamshire. Le gang avait dérobé 2,5 millions de livres dans le train de nuit postal qui ralliait Londres à Glasgow.

August 1966. London East End gang leaders Ronnie and Reggie Kray take tea at home. The twin brothers ran 'the Firm', specializing in protection rackets, illegal gambling and drinking clubs, and ultimately murder. They were each jailed for 30 years in 1969.

August 1966. Die Bandenchefs des Londoner East End, Ronnie und Reggie Kray beim Tee. Die Zwillingsbrüder betrieben ihre eigene „Firma", die sich auf Erpressung von Schutzgeldern, illegalem Glücksspiel, Nachtbars und Mord spezialisiert hatte. Sie wurden 1969 zu je 30 Jahren Gefängnis verurteilt.

Août 1966. Ronnie et Reggie Kay, chefs d'un gang de l'Est de Londres, prenant leur thé à la maison. Les deux frères jumeaux géraient la « Firme », spécialisée dans la couverture de rackets, les salles de jeux et clubs illégaux et, plus tard, le meurtre. Ils furent condamnés à 30 ans de prison en 1969.

The *Torrey Canyon* disaster. In March 1967 a giant oil tanker ran aground on rocks between the Scilly Isles and Land's End, Cornwall. In an attempt to prevent pollution spreading, the RAF bombed the wreck (above), before she finally sank (left) in April.

Die Katastrophe der *Torrey Canyon*. Im März 1967 lief der riesige Öltanker zwischen den Scilly-Inseln und Land's End vor Cornwall auf ein Riff auf. Die Royal Air Force warf Bomben auf das Schiffswrack ab (oben), um die Ausbreitung des Ölteppichs zu verhindern. Im April sank der Tanker (links) schließlich.

La catastrophe du *Torrey Canyon*. En mars 1967, un pétrolier géant s'échoua entre les îles de Scilly et Land's End en Cournouailles. Pour éviter que la pollution ne se propage, l'armée de l'air britannique bombarda l'épave (ci-dessus) qui finit par couler (à gauche) en avril.

Soldiers (above) in the city of Skopje, former Yogoslavia, dig for bodies in the ruins after the earthquake, August 1963. (Right) Nikita Khrushchev, Soviet premier, and Josip Tito, President of Yugoslavia, stand in front of the shattered Army Club in Skopje.

In der vom Erdbeben verwüsteten Stadt Skopje, ehemals Jugoslawien, suchen Soldaten (oben) in den Ruinen nach Überlebenden, August 1963. (Rechts) Der sowjetische Staatschef Nikita Chruschtschow und Jugoslawiens Staatschef Josip Tito stehen vor einem zerstörten Haus der Armee in Skopje.

Des soldats (ci-dessus) dans la ville de Skopje, ex-Yougoslavie, creusent pour retrouver des corps sous les ruines, août 1963. (A droite) Nikita Khrouchtchev, le premier secrétaire soviétique, et Josip Tito, le président de la Yougoslavie, devant les ruines de la maison de l'armée de Skopje.

13. All human life
Menschliches, Allzumenschliches
Les petits et les grands événements de la vie

A two-man sky taxi in flight, somewhere just over
America, 4 July 1967. It was invented by W F Moore and
developed by Textron's Bell Aerosystems Company,
Buffalo, New York. It was intended for moon exploration.

Ein Zwei-Mann-Sky-Taxi fliegt irgendwo über Amerika,
4. Juli 1967. Die Maschine stammte von W. F. Moore,
und die Entwicklung übernahm die amerikanische Firma
für Weltraumtechnik Textron's Bell, Buffalo, New York.
Sie war für Mondexkursionen vorgesehen.

Taxi volant à deux places, en plein vol quelque part
aux Etats-Unis, 4 juillet 1967. Cet engin fut inventé par
W. F. Moore et élaboré par la compagnie Bell Aerosystems
de Textron, Buffalo, New York. Il avait été conçu pour
explorer la lune.

13. All human life
Menschliches, Allzumenschliches
Les petits et les grands événements de la vie

However dramatic the happenings on the international scene in the Sixties, there was still time for ordinary people to do extraordinary things, and for the camera to be there to record them.

People invented strange contests – to see who could cram the most bodies into a telephone kiosk, to leap the widest chasm on a motorbike, to cross rivers and oceans in the strangest craft. Others sought to trick the general public in novel ways. A hoaxer named Alan Abel persuaded the American public that a topless, female string quartet would provide concertgoers with a 'purer sound'.

Researchers for the US Navy announced that the bottle-nosed dolphin had a superior brain to human beings. The US Air Force dismissed the many sightings of alleged UFOs as being probably 'astronomical' in origin. Ham, the first 'astrochimp', was rewarded with an apple after being shot 150 miles into space. Lenny Bruce, the US nightclub comedian, was charged with obscenity.

The Houston Astrodome was opened in April 1965, as the world's biggest covered arena. It was designed to be used as a baseball field. The air-conditioning was fine, but it was impossible for the fielders to spot the baseball against the background of roof panels.

Bei all den dramatischen Ereignissen, die sich auf internationaler Ebene in den sechziger Jahren abspielten, blieb dennoch genügend Zeit für außergewöhnliche Dinge gewöhnlicher Menschen und die Kamera, um dies wiederum aufzuzeichnen.

Die Menschen kamen auf seltsame Ideen – es ging darum, so viele Menschen wie möglich in eine Telefonzelle zu quetschen, die breiteste Schlucht mit dem Motorrad zu überspringen oder Flüsse und Ozeane mit den eigenartigsten Vehikeln zu überqueren. Andere versuchten die Öffentlichkeit auf immer neuere Art und Weise an der Nase herumzuführen. Die Zeitungsente,

Alan Abel, sollte den Amerikanern weismachen, daß man als Konzertbesucher ein „besseres Klangerlebnis" habe, wenn ein Damenstreichquartett oben ohne auftreten würde.

Forscher der US-Navy verkündeten, daß der Große Tümmler, eine Delphinart, über eine höhere Intelligenz verfügt als der Mensch. Die US-Luftwaffe tat die angeblichen Beobachtungen von außerirdischen UFOs als wahrscheinlich „astronomische" Erscheinungen ab. Ham, der erste Schimpanse im Weltraum, wurde mit einem Apfel belohnt, nachdem man ihn zuvor 240 Kilometer weit in den Weltraum geschossen hatte. Lenny Bruce, der amerikanische Nachtclub-Komiker; wurde die Verletzung der guten Sitten vorgeworfen.

Im April 1965 wurde in Houston die weltgrößte überdachte Sportarena, das Astrodome, eröffnet. Sie war für Baseball-Spiele konzipiert. Die Klimaanlage funktionierte perfekt, doch es war den Spieler unmöglich, den Ball vor den gemusterten Dachverstrebungen zu erkennen.

Les années soixante furent secouées par toutes sortes d'événements dramatiques sur la scène internationale. Ce qui n'empêcha pas à des gens ordinaires d'accomplir des choses extra-ordinaires et à un appareil de photo d'en conserver la trace.

On inventa des concours farfelus. C'était à qui entasserait le plus de gens dans une cabine téléphonique, à qui franchirait le plus grand obstacle en moto, à qui traverserait les mers et les océans dans la plus invraisemblable des embarcations. Il y avait aussi ceux qui innovaient en la manière de tromper les gens. Un mauvais plaisantin nommé Alan Abel réussit à convaincre le public américain qu'un quatuor à cordes de femmes jouant seins nus offrirait aux auditeurs un « son plus pur ».

Des chercheurs de la marine américaine annoncèrent que l'intelligence du dauphin était supérieure à celle de l'homme. L'armée de l'air américaine rejeta les nombreuses allégations selon lesquelles les Ovnis auraient pu être d'origine « astronomique ». Ham, le premier singe de l'espace, fut récompensé d'une pomme pour avoir parcouru près de 240 kilomètres dans l'espace. Lenny Bruce, le comique américain des boîtes de nuit, fut accusé d'outrages aux bonnes moeurs.

L'astrodôme d'Houston fut inauguré en avril 1965 comme étant le plus grand stade couvert du monde. Il avait été conçu pour accueillir des matchs de base-ball. L'air conditionné fonctionnait parfaitement mais il était impossible aux joueurs de distinguer la balle des panneaux qui recouvraient le plafond.

October 1961.
The Goodyear
Illuminated Tyre.
The tyre was
illuminated by a
series of light bulbs
inside the wheel rim.

Oktober 1961. Der
beleuchtete Reifen
von Goodyear. Eine
Reihe von Glüh-
birnen wurden im
Reifenrand installiert
und ließen das Rad
hell erleuchten.

Octobre 1961. Le
pneu illuminé de
Goodyear. Ce pneu
était illuminé au
moyen d'ampoules
intégrées dans la
jante de la roue.

Not as clear as hand signals... An attempt to break the record for the greatest number of people successfully crammed into a Morris Mini car, 1966.

Nicht so eindeutig wie ein Handzeichen ... Ein Versuch, den Rekord so viele Menschen wie möglich in einen Morris Mini unterzubringen, zu brechen, 1966.

Pas aussi clair qu'un signe de la main ... Tentative pour battre le record du plus grand nombre de gens entassés dans une Morris Mini, 1966.

February 1965.
Robert and Eileen
Greenhill (née
Pettigrew) pose for
photographs outside
the Church of St
John the Evangelist,
Notting Hill,
London.

Februar 1965.
Robert und Eileen
Greenhill (geborene
Pettigrew) stellen
sich vor der Kirche
von St. John in
Notting Hill,
London, den
Fotografen.

Février 1965. Robert
et Eileen Greenhill
(née Pettigrew)
posent pour les
photographes devant
l'église de Saint Jean
de l'Evangile,
Notting Hill,
Londres.

New York, 1966. A
couple demonstrate
the body's ability to
function as an
electrical conductor
at a lecture
sponsored by the
Atomic Energy
Commission.

New York, 1966. Ein
Paar demonstriert
während eines Vor-
trags, der von der
Atomenergiebehörde
abgehalten wurde,
daß der menschliche
Körper als elektri-
scher Leiter fun-
gieren kann.

New York, 1966.
Ce couple fait une
démonstration
prouvant que le
corps peut servir de
conducteur électrique
lors d'une conférence
sponsorisée par la
Commission pour
l'énergie atomique.

A handful of fun. Customers enjoy drinks at a high
kitsch 'funfair house' in Munich, 1969.

Jede Menge Spaß. Gäste amüsieren sich bei einem
Drink in einem hochgradig kitschigen Vergnügungs-
lokal in München, 1969.

Jeux de mains. Des clients ravis de boire un verre
dans un bar particulièrement kitsch de Munich, 1969.

Public privacy in
The Bed Bar,
Frankfurt's latest
night-spot,
January 1961.

Privatsphäre in der
Öffentlichkeit in der
Bed Bar, der am
längsten geöffneten
Nachtbar Frankfurts,
Januar 1961.

Intimité en public
au Bed Bar de
Francfort, la der-
nière boîte de nuit à
la mode, janvier
1961.

Profit from temptation. Hugh Hefner arrives at London Airport, June 1966. Hefner was editor of the *Playboy Magazine*, and owner of the string of Playboy Clubs. By the Sixties he had become a multimillionaire.

Profit mit der Versuchung. Hugh Hefner bei seiner Ankunft auf dem Londoner Flughafen, Juni 1966. Hefner war der Herausgeber des Magazins *Playboy* und der Eigentümer einer Kette von Playboy-Clubs. In den sechziger Jahren war er bereits Multimillionär.

Succombez à la tentation. Hugh Hefner à son arrivée à l'aéroport de Londres, juin 1966. Directeur du magazine *Playboy* et propriétaire d'une série de clubs Playboy, Hefner devint multimillionnaire dans les années soixante.

Prophet of forgiveness. Billy Graham shakes hands with the faithful, 1966. Graham's preaching crusades around the world are reckoned to have brought millions of people to adopt the Christian faith.

Prophet der Vergebung. Billy Graham schüttelt den Gläubigen die Hände, 1966. Graham hatte auf seinen Gebetskreuzfahrten um die ganze Welt Millionen von Menschen vom christlichen Glauben überzeugt.

Prophète du pardon. Billy Graham serrant la main de fidèles, 1966. Les croisades du prédicateur à travers le monde auraient contribué à la conversion de millions de gens à la religion chrétienne.

Hear no evil... Three Metropolitan Water Board inspectors use sounding sticks to listen for leaks in the water pipes beneath Rosebery Avenue, Finsbury, London, 1966. The simple device, a piece of solid ash with a beech earpiece, was better than any electronic gadget.

Man hört nichts ... Drei Beamte der städtischen Wasseraufsichtsbehörde horchen mit Holzröhrchen die Rosebery Avenue nach Löchern in den Wasserrohren ab, Finsbury, London, 1966. Dieses einfache Instrument, ein Stück festes Eschenholz und ein Buchenstückchen eignet sich besser dafür als jeder andere elektronische Apparat.

Esprit, es-tu là? Trois inspecteurs de la compagnie des eaux utilisent des sondes en bois pour localiser les fuites d'une canalisation sur Rosebery Avenue, Finsbury, Londres, 1966. Cet instrument tout simple, une baguette de frêne avec un écouteur en hêtre, était plus efficace qu'un gadget électronique.

...See no evil. West Berliners peer through the newly built Berlin Wall into the Eastern Sector near Checkpoint Charlie, October 1966.

Man sieht nichts ... Westberliner spähen in der Nähe des berühmten Check-point Charlie durch die neugebaute Berliner Mauer in den Ostteil der Stadt hinüber, Oktober 1966.

Esprit, où es-tu? Près de Checkpoint Charlie, des Berlinois de l'Ouest jettent un regard à l'Est à travers le mur de Berlin récemment construit, octobre 1966.

Waiter on the water. An Austrian waiter leaves
a harbourside hotel and speeds along on water
skis to deliver an order, 1969.

Kellner auf dem Wasser. Dieser österreichische
Kellner schwingt sich auf die Wasserski und
prescht an einem Hafenhotel entlang, um
einem Gast seine Bestellung zu bringen, 1969.

Garçon de café sur l'eau. Un serveur autrichien
d'un hôtel du port, très pressé, apporte sa
commande en skis nautiques, 1969.

Sergeant Major Tom Gledhill leaps over 20 members of the Royal Artillery on his BSA A50 twin motorcycle, March 1966. Honestly!

Hauptfeldwebel Tom Gledhill springt mit seiner BSA A50 über 20 Mitglieder der Königlichen Artillerie, März 1966. Tatsächlich!

Le sergent-major Tom Gledhill saute par-dessus 20 artilleurs britanniques avec sa moto à deux cylindres BSA A50, mars 1966. Franchement!

The wrong man.
Pressmen snap Toralf
Engan of Norway
(foreground)
assuming he has
won the Olympic
ski jump event at
Innsbruck, 1964.
The real winner is
Veikko Kankkonen
of Finland
(background).

Der falsche Mann.
Ein Schnellschuß für
die Presse von Toralf
Engan aus Nor-
wegen (im Vorder-
grund), der bei den
Olympischen Win-
terspielen von
Innsbruck, glaubte,
er habe das Ski-
springen gewonnen,
1964. Der Gewinner
war Veikko Kank-
konen aus Finnland
(im Hintergrund).

Erreur sur la
personne. La presse
photographie le
Norvégien Toralf
Engan (au premier
plan) pensant qu'il
vient de gagner
l'épreuve olympique
du saut à ski à
Innsbruck, 1964.
Le vrai vainqueur
est le Finlandais
Veikko Kankkonen
(à l'arrière-plan).

November 1965.
A high speed
water-skiing team
demonstrate the
'flying high and
dry' stunt at the
Cypress Gardens,
Florida, USA.

November 1965.
Wasserskifahrer
demonstrieren in
Cypress Gardens,
Florida, eindrucks-
voll, wie man über
dem Wasser „hoch
und trocken" fliegen
kann.

Novembre 1965.
Equipe de skieurs
nautiques en pleine
exécution d'un
numéro de haute
voltige aux Cypress
Gardens, Floride,
Etats-Unis.

May 1963. Sixteen-year-old trainee chef Peter Maddox of
Hollingsworth, Cheshire, practises fire-eating at home, as his mother
and nine-month-old brother look on. The soufflé was ruined.

Mai 1963. Der 16 Jahre alte Peter Maddox aus Hollingsworth,
Cheshire, Auszubildener zum Küchenchef, übt sich als Feuer-
schlucker, während seine Mutter und sein neun Monate
alter Bruder zusehen. Das Soufflé war auf jeden Fall ruiniert.

Hollingsworth, Cheshire, mai 1963. Cet apprenti cuisinier de
16 ans, Peter Maddox, accomplit un numéro de cracheur de feu
sous les yeux de sa mère et de son frère âgé de neuf mois. Tant
pis pour le soufflé au four.

The best of British beef. Farmer Colin Newlove rides his four-year-old
Yorkshire bull through a burning hoop. The stunt took place on
Newlove's farm in the village of Bugthorpe, Yorkshire, August 1963.

Ein gutes Stück englisches Rindfleisch. Der Farmer Colin Newlove
springt auf seinem vierjährigen Yorkshire-Bullen durch einen bren-
nenden Reifen. Das Kunststück fand auf seinem Hof in der Ortschaft
Bugthorpe, Yorkshire, statt, August 1963.

Le meilleur du boeuf britannique. L'agricole Colin Newlove et son
taureau du Yorkshire, âgé de quatre ans, sautent avec brio au travers
d'un cercle de feu. Newlove exécuta cette cascade non loin de sa
ferme à Bugthorpe, un village du Yorkshire, août 1963.

November 1965. A good head for drinking…
A man and woman enjoy a drink while they
test a pair of head-massaging machines.

November 1965. Beim Trinken muß man
einen klaren Kopf behalten … Diese Dame
und dieser Herr genießen ihre Drinks, während sie gleichzeitig Kopfmassagegeräte testen.

Novembre 1965. Une tête à boire des
verres … Madame et Monsieur boivent un
verre tout en testant une machine prodiguant
des massages de la tête.

Taking the car for a run... The British athlete Bruce Tulloh uses a breathing hose while Dr Griffith Pugh (inside car) monitor's Tulloh's physical stress and endurance, 1966.

Zum Laufen sollte man ein Auto benutzen ... Der britische Sportler Bruce Tulloh versorgt sich über einen Atmungsschlauch mit Sauerstoff. Dr. Griffith Pugh (im Auto) sitzt und mißt über einen Monitor den Streßpegel und die Ausdauer des Läufers, 1966.

Prendre la voiture pour aller courir ... L'athlète britannique Bruce Tulloh court avec cet appareil respiratoire tandis que le docteur Griffith Pugh (à l'intérieur de la voiture) enregistre les courbes d'endurance et de stress physique de Tulloh, 1966.

Prince binned. Charles, Prince of Wales, in a sketch called 'Scoop', part of the Trinity College Dryden Society revue *Revolution*, Cambridge, February 1969.

Der Prinz im Eimer. Prinz Charles von Wales spielt in dem Sketch „Scoop", Teil der Revue *Revolution*, der Trinity College Dryden Society, Cambridge, Februar 1969.

Un prince en boîte. Charles, prince de Galles, dans un sketch intitulé « Scoop » qui faisait partie du spectacle *Revolution* donné par l'association Dryden du Trinity College, Cambridge, février 1969.

Duke stunned. The Duke of Windsor (centre) and singer Jane Pickens
Langley react as Floyd Patterson knocks out Ingemar Johansson to retain
his world heavyweight title, Miami Beach, 14 March 1961.

Der fassungslose Herzog. Dem Herzog von Windsor (Mitte) und der Sängerin Jane Pickens Langley steht die Verblüffung ins Gesicht geschrieben, als
Floyd Patterson seinen Gegner Ingemar Johansson im Kampf um den Titel
im Schwergewicht niederschlägt, Miami Beach, 14. März 1961.

Un duc ébahi. Le duc de Windsor (au centre) et la chanteuse Jane Pickens
Langley retiennent leur souffle tandis que Floyd Patterson met K.-O.
Ingemar Johansson pour conserver son titre de champion des poids lourds,
Miami Beach, 14 mars 1961.

Hand to hand... A postman stationed outside a post office in Washington,
USA, collects tax returns from car drivers, April 1965. The drivers were
rushing to beat the midnight deadline for submission.

Von Hand zu Hand ... Ein Postangestellter im Außendienst sammelt die
Steuererklärungen direkt von den Autofahrern ein, April 1965. Die Fahrer
waren in großer Eile, um den Abgabetermin vor Mitternacht einzuhalten.

De main à main ... Ce postier recueille devant une poste de Washington
les déclarations d'impôts que des automobilistes viennent déposer en toute
hâte avant minuit, dernier délai pour le dépôt des déclarations, avril 1965.

Door to door...
A salesman
demonstrates his
wares to a
housewife in Bootle,
Lancashire,
November 1967.

Von Tür zu Tür ...
Ein Handelsreisen-
der zeigt einer
Hausfrau in Bootle,
Lancashire, sein
Warensortiment,
November 1967.

De porte à porte ...
Ce représentant
présente ses produits
à une ménagère de
Bootle, Lancashire,
novembre 1967.

Odd driver…
Alan Band's bizarre
photograph of
what appears to be
a strangely shod
Alsatian, 1965.

Ein eigenartiger
Fahrer … Das
witzige Foto von
Alan Bands zeigt,
wie ein Schäferhund
mit Schuhen aus-
sieht, 1965.

Un drôle de conduc-
teur … Alan Band
a photographié ce
berger allemand
curieusement
chaussé, 1965.

Odd passenger… Captain J Edwards
fastens the seatbelt on one of his pet
alligators, May 1963.

Ein seltsamer Fahrgast … Polizeihauptmann
J. Edwards legt seinem Babyalligator den
Sicherheitsgurt an, Mai 1963.

Un drôle de passager … Le capitaine
J. Edwards attache la ceinture de son
animal familier, un alligator, mai 1963.

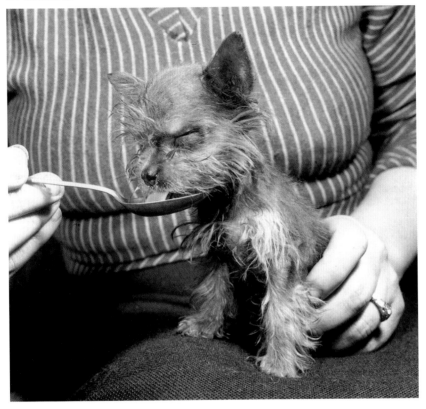

Lap dog... One of the smallest breeds in the
world takes a drink from a spoon, March 1960.

Schoßhündchen ... Ein Löffel voll Wasser genügt
für dieses Hündchen, das zu den kleinsten
Hunderassen der Welt gehört, März 1960.

Sur les genoux ... Ce chien qui appartient à une
des races les plus petites au monde boit à la
cuillère, mars 1960.

Well-padded seat... A dog's-eye view of two chihuahuas and their owners, waiting
for the judges' verdict at the Cruft's Dog Show at London's Olympia, February 1967.

Ein gutgepolstertes Sitzkissen ... Aus dem Blickwinkel dieser beiden Chihuahuas.
Die Hunde und ihre Besitzerinnen warten auf das Ergebnis auf der großen Cruft's-
Hundeparade im Olympia, London, Februar 1967.

Un siège bien rempli ... Deux chihuahuas et leurs maîtresses, vues à hauteur de chien,
attendent le verdict du jury à l'issue du concours pour chiens de Cruft à l'Olympia de
Londres, février 1967.

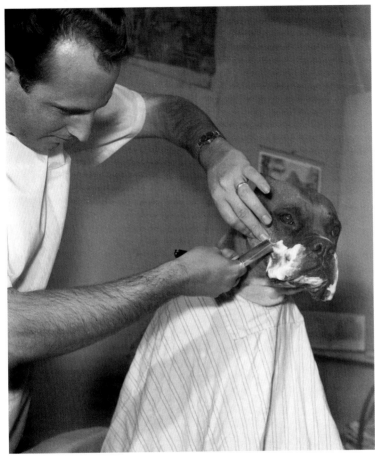

Hair loss. Fritz,
a television celebrity
bulldog, is shaved by
a Californian barber,
April 1961.

Haarlos. Die
berühmte Fernseh-
Bulldogge Fritz muß
bei einem Friseur in
Kalifornien Haare
lassen, April 1961.

Des poils en moins.
Le bulldog Fritz,
une vedette du petit
écran, entre les
mains d'un coiffeur
californien, avril
1961.

Hair gain. An
Amsterdam dog
models a wig
made by a Dutch
hairdresser,
November 1962.

Kunsthaar. Ein
Amsterdamer Hund
sitzt mit einer Pe-
rücke für einen
holländischen
Friseur Modell,
November 1962.

Des cheveux en
plus. Ce chien
d'Amsterdam
présente une
perruque conçue
par un coiffeur
hollandais,
novembre 1962.

Index

How to buy or license a picture from this book

The pictures in this book are drawn from the extensive archives of The Hulton Getty Picture Collection, originally formed in 1947 as the Hulton Press Library. The Collection contains approximately 15 million images, some of which date from the earliest days of photography. It includes original material from leading press agencies – Topical Press, Keystone, Central Press, Fox Photos and General Photographic Agency as well as from *Picture Post*, the *Daily Express* and the *Evening Standard*. Pictures in this book which are from other sources are listed on page 398.

Picture Licensing Information

To license the pictures listed below, except any marked *, please call Getty Images + 44 171 266 2662 or email info@getty-images.com your picture selection with the page/reference numbers.

Hulton Getty Online

All of the pictures listed below and countless others are available via Hulton Getty Online at: http://www.hultongetty.com

Buying a print

For details of how to purchase exhibition-quality prints call The Hulton Getty Picture Gallery + 44 171 376 4525 (fax) + 44 171 376 4524 hulton.gallery@getty-images.com

Acknowledgements

Alan Band 138-9, 141, 286, 388
Peter Ferraz 116, 119
Gamma Liaison 220/Front cover
Ernst Haas Studio 87
The Observer 39, 43, 45, 58, 62,
    66-9, 82-3, 106, 115, 117, 118,
    120-1, 127, 142, 145, 159, 164,
    169, 171-3, 183, 208, 211,
    217-19, 233, 262, 267, 270, 298,
    309, 333, 338, 387

Pictures from other sources

Robert Hunt Library
    Frontispiece, 102, 353

Topham Picturepoint
    28, 31, 165, 167, 253, 291